Your
Rewards
in
Heaven

Your Rewards in Heaven

MAX M. RICE

ACCENT BOOKS
Denver, Colorado

ACCENT BOOKS
A division of Accent Publications, Inc.
12100 W. Sixth Avenue
P.O. Box 15337
Denver, Colorado 80215

Library of Congress Catalog Card Number: 80-68885

ISBN 0-89636-063-6

To my father, Max Rice, Sr.
To my wife, Vivian
To my children, Vivian and Tim Wilson,
Carolyn and Eunice Rice
who helped make this book possible.

Look-Up Lodge and Camp, a Christian retreat center of which Author Max M. Rice is Director, is located at Travelers Rest, South Carolina.

Contents

1
Rewards in Heaven

Join me in your imagination for the biggest TV game show of all time: The $25 Million Dollar Ball Blast. A contestant sits on a stool and the Master of Ceremonies fires the Ball Blast Cannon. Large, colorful plastic balls zoom toward the contestant at intervals. Each ball contains a certificate for a fabulous prize, such as a life income of $50,000 a year, a mansion, or a new automobile each year. If the contestant is able to catch a ball and drop it into a basket, that prize is his.

Contestant A is in place. The balls begin to fly. Just before he reaches for the first one, he notices that there is a more comfortable chair in the wings. He rushes to get it. While in the wings he notices some of the crew enjoying cans of soft drinks. Never one to miss such an opportunity, he has one with the boys.

Rushing back with his softer chair, he catches a glimpse of himself in a mirror. His hair has become disheveled. He finds a comb and brush and makes himself presentable. Finally he is ready to start catching balls, but time is called. The Master of Ceremonies has substituted another contestant.

Contestant B doesn't particularly like the stool either, but so what? He is so excited about the game that he hardly notices the stool is hard. As ball after ball goes into the basket, he is oblivious to his looks. The gong sounds. He is tired and disheveled, but his basket is full.

Which would you consider to be the more successful contestant? Suppose you heard a couple discussing the show. One said, "A was the most successful person ever to appear on the show. No other guest ever took care of himself so well."

Would you agree, or would you consider the few brief moments A was better off than B to be inconsequential compared to the many years B would enjoy the prizes? Doubtless, you would be tempted to say to A, "You fool!"

Of course, compared to eternity, life on this earth is infinitely less than a half-hour game show would be to the contestant's earthly life span. And the consequences of a wasted life are infinitely greater.

Many Christians are surprised to learn that there will be tremendous differences in heaven. "If all are perfect, how can we be different?" "If I have to face throughout eternity the results of a wasted life, how can I be happy?" "Won't my sins be forgiven?"

Others feel that the promise of rewards is not a worthy motive. They have heard people accused of being so heavenly minded that they are of no earthly good. The promise of "pie in the sky by and by" has been used as an excuse for lack of social action.

Questions such as these cause many to ignore the numerous Scriptures which clearly teach that the promise of heavenly rewards can be a worthy motive for our service for the Lord in this life. These questions and others will be dealt with in the next chapter. But first let us take a look at heaven, as the Bible reveals it, and then consider Scriptures which clearly teach that you "can take it with you." That is, what we do or fail to do in this life will carry forward to the next.

What the Bible Teaches About Heaven

"Today shalt thou be with me in paradise," Jesus said to the thief on the cross beside Him who acknowledged Jesus as Lord and himself as one justly condemned and needing mercy (Luke 23:42-43). Jesus evidently spoke of a place where He expected to be before the day was out.

The Apostle Paul, without question speaking of himself, said that he knew of a man who was caught up into paradise, and he designated the place as the "third heaven." Paul said, in II Corinthians 12:2-4:

> I knew a man in Christ above fourteen years ago, (whether in the body, I cannot tell: or whether out of the body, I cannot tell: God knoweth;) such an one caught up to the third heaven.
> And I knew such a man ... How that he was caught up into paradise, and heard unspeakable words, which it is not lawful for a man to utter.

We learn, then, from the unimpeachable witness of the Lord Jesus Christ and the Apostle Paul that heaven is paradise and is a definite place. We can also conclude that the place heaven is "up" from the earth.

YOUR REWARDS IN HEAVEN

The first statement in the Bible tells us that God created the heavens and the earth, and the Hebrew word for *heaven* is in the plural. In the hundreds of times the word *heaven* is used in the Bible it may refer to one of three major realms:

(1) *The atmospheric heaven.* This is the blanket of air which surrounds the earth, extending about twenty miles above the earth.

(2) *The celestial heaven.* This is the sphere in which the sun and moon and the stars appear— "the lights in the firmament of the heaven to divide the day from the night" (Genesis 1:14).

(3) *The heaven of heavens.* This "third heaven" is evidently the abode of God. While fully acknowledging the omnipresence of God, whereby He fills heaven and earth (Jeremiah 23:23) and there is no possibility for anyone to flee from His presence (Psalm 139:7-10) because He is everywhere, the Bible teaches that this heaven has been God's dwelling place and throne ever since it was created.

What would such a place be like?

In preparation for writing his great prophetic book, Revelation, the Apostle John was given a glimpse of the throne in heaven and the One who sat upon it. In the magnificent description he gives of this experience in Revelation 4, we see celestial beings, not resting day and night, saying, "Holy, holy, holy, Lord God Almighty, which was, and is, and is to come" (verse 8). And redeemed beings worship Him:

> The four and twenty elders fall down before him that sat on the throne, and worship him that liveth for ever and ever, and cast their crowns before the throne, saying, Thou art worthy, O Lord, to receive glory and honour and power: for thou hast created all things, and for thy pleasure they are and were created (verses 10-11).

Stephen, in his defense of his faith just before he was martyred, said:

> Howbeit the most High dwelleth not in temples made with hands; as saith the prophet, Heaven is my throne, and earth is my footstool . . ." (Acts 7:48-49).

We know that the Lord Jesus Christ is in heaven. While here on earth Jesus spoke often about heaven. In the last few days before His death, He told His disciples repeatedly that He would soon be going to His Father; for example, "I go unto my Father" (John 14:12) and "If ye loved me, ye would rejoice, because I said, I go unto the Father . . ." (John 14:28).

Luke records Christ's ascension into heaven (Acts 1:8-11). Hebrews 10:12, 13 gives us the picture of Christ in heaven today:

But this man, after he had offered one sacrifice for sins for ever, sat down on the right hand of God; From henceforth expecting till his enemies be made his footstool.

There, in heaven, Christ's work on our behalf as the great High Priest is shown in Hebrews 7:25: "He ever liveth to make intercession for them."

With God the Most High and Jesus Christ our Saviour, together with the host of celestial beings and all the redeemed of the ages living in heaven, what a glorious future life awaits every Christian! The Bible assures us that we have a home waiting for us, eternal in the heavens:

For we know that if our earthly house of this tabernacle were dissolved, we have a building of God, an house not made with hands, eternal in the heavens . . . Therefore, we are always confident, knowing that, whilst we are at home in the body, we are absent from the Lord . . . We are confident, I say, and willing rather to be absent from the body, and to be present with the Lord (II Corinthians 5:1-8).

Rewarded for Our Works

Oddly enough, we are told very little more than this—that we are to be present with the Lord—from the time we go to heaven by death until the time of resurrection and we stand in our resurrection bodies before Christ to be judged for how we have lived as Christians.

Speaking to believers, the Apostle Paul told them:

> For we must all appear before the judgment seat of Christ; that every one may receive the things done in his body, according to that he hath done, whether it be good or bad (II Corinthians 5:10).

The purpose of our being judged by Christ is not for Him to judge or condemn us for our sins, because our sins were judged at the cross when He died in our place. Here we are judged for our service for Him during the time we live on earth as Christians. Paul, writing as he often did in the analogy of an athletic contest, saw the faithful Christian rewarded with incorruptible crowns for running the race of life well.

How You Live Now Will Make a Difference

The Bible leaves no room to doubt that we will be judged by our deeds and how we live our Christian lives will make a difference in our eternal rewards. But don't confuse the judgment of works, which determines our rewards, with the judgment of faith, which determines our salvation. Comparing the two should be helpful.

YOUR REWARDS IN HEAVEN

Saved by Faith

For by grace are ye saved through faith; and that not of yourselves: it is the gift of God: Not of works, lest any man should boast (Ephesians 2:8-9).

But to him that worketh not, but believeth on him that justifieth the ungodly, his faith is counted for righteousness (Romans 4:5).

Therefore we conclude that a man is justified by faith without the deeds of the law (Romans 3:28).

Rewards for Works

And, behold, I come quickly; and my reward is with me, to give every man according as his work shall be (Revelation 22:12).

For the Son of man shall come in the glory of his Father with his angels; and then he shall reward every man according to his works (Matthew 16:27).

Who will render to every man according to his deeds (Romans 2:6).

For we must all appear before the judgment seat of Christ; that every one may receive the things done in his body, according to that he hath done, whether it be good or bad (II Corinthians 5:10).

Do, however, be sure of your salvation by grace before considering eternal rewards in heaven.

There are many, many good people—moral and even religious—who are not sure they are going to heaven. Some do not even know they need to do anything to prepare themselves for heaven. If you should be one of these, the Righteous and Just Judge of the world of Romans 2, quoted above, would have to render your deeds as worthless because you have not accepted the salvation He has provided for you. None of your good deeds, none of your good works, even if you worked in a church, are a "ticket to heaven."

To be "saved by grace" means that we, all of us born into the human family, are sinners by the very nature we inherited from Adam. We can never be good enough for heaven, for there is no sin there. We deserve the punishment for sin—death (Romans 3:23 and 6:23). But Jesus Christ, the perfect Son of God, took upon Himself our sin and received our punishment—death on the cross. If we accept what Christ did for us, God declares us "not guilty." That is why, when we put our faith in Christ, we have accepted the gift of salvation from God and we are saved "by grace through faith." It is by grace because we did not deserve it. It is through faith because we believed and accepted.

If you have accepted Jesus Christ as your Saviour, and have been born again as John 3:3 says we must be, you are bound for heaven.

As you read of eternal rewards, remember that we also receive blessings as Christians in this life.

These blessings may come either from God, from men, or from the natural result of good living. However, life on this earth is so short compared to eternity that earthly rewards are of relatively little importance. In fact, in the following passage Jesus teaches us that we should not show kindnesses to others for the sake of being rewarded in kind in this life; we can leave such rewards up to Christ at the resurrection:

> Then said he also to him that bade him, When thou makest a dinner or a supper, call not thy friends, nor thy brethren, neither thy kinsmen, nor thy rich neighbours; lest they also bid thee again, and a recompence be made thee. But when thou makest a feast, call the poor, the maimed, the lame, the blind: And thou shalt be blessed; for they cannot recompense thee: for thou shalt be recompensed at the resurrection of the just (Luke 14:12-14).

Differences in Heaven

For the purposes of this study, Biblical teachings on differences in heaven are divided into six different categories as follows:

(1) Rewards which repay many times over for losses or sufferings we endure because of Christ.

(2) Rewards or treasures for good deeds and sacrificial service.

(3) Varying amounts of authority or rule based on our faithfulness.

(4) Greatness in heaven based on humility, servant spirit, and obedience.

(5) Place of honor based on purity.

(6) Mercy received based on mercy given.

Note in each category how faith in God as a rewarder would make very practical differences in our lives.

1. *Rewards for Sufferings or Losses*

God promises to repay us many times over for all losses, sufferings, persecutions, or sacrifices caused by our loyalty to Christ. Jesus said:

Blessed are they which are persecuted for righteousness' sake: for theirs is the kingdom of heaven. Blessed are ye, when men shall revile you, and persecute you, and shall say all manner of evil against you falsely, for my sake. Rejoice, and be exceeding glad: for great is your reward in heaven: for so persecuted they the prophets which were before you (Matthew 5:10-12).

The nature of these rewards is not revealed. It is clear, however, that they are so wonderful that they should cause great rejoicing.

Suppose I told you that if you worked in my yard all day, I would give you a great reward. After a hard day's work, I gave you a penny. You would think I was rather cheap, wouldn't you? Is God

21

cheap? Do you think we will be disappointed in Him when we discover what His great rewards are? We can be certain that all through eternity we will consider the great reward to be truly great.

How do you feel when people insult you, persecute you, lie about you, and speak evil of you because of your Christian stand? The Bible says we should rejoice because our reward in heaven is great (Matthew 5:12).

I once shared this verse with a group of eight-year-old campers at Look-Up Lodge. A counselor told me he later heard one camper insult another. The insulted camper put out his hand and said, "Thank you. You just got me a reward in heaven." Of course, he not only got a reward in heaven but also was rewarded on the spot. Had he not had faith, the ugly remark would have ruined his day. As a result of faith, he had a happy day.

Do you sulk, feel sorry for yourself, or get upset because of persecution? Are you unwilling to take a strong Christian stand because of fear of other people? If so, examine your faith in the promises of God.

In Mark 10:29-30, Jesus promises a hundredfold return in this life plus eternal blessing if we give up home, loved ones, or property for Him. This is like someone telling you, "Give me a dollar now and I will give you a hundred dollars next week." What would you do? If you did not give him the dollar, that would be strong evidence that you did not believe him. Do people who do not invest in heavenly treasures really believe God?

Jim attended a Christian retreat. Though some of the people were strangers, he felt an immediate bond of fellowship. He was included in a wonderful weekend because he was a Christian.

But the next weekend, he was excluded because he was a Christian. A group from his office went deer hunting. Because they planned to spend the evening drinking and telling dirty jokes, Jim was left out. How should he feel? Great! God will make it up. This is why a Christian can't lose for winning. When we are included in good Christian fellowship, we are happy. When we are excluded because of our stand, we are even happier. God is going to repay us a hundred times in this life and infinitely more in eternity.

Often teenagers discover that they must give up their boyfriends or girlfriends because the Bible says, "Be ye not unequally yoked together with unbelievers" (II Corinthians 6:14). How should they feel? Great! Why? Because God will make it up to them one hundred times in this life and throughout eternity. Does this mean He will give them a hundred boy- or girlfriends? Perhaps. But, more likely, He will lead them to one a hundred times better.

It's easy for adults to see that the teenager should obey God regardless of how difficult it seems at the time. But what about adult situations? Are we willing to give up a more lucrative income in order to have more time to serve God? Is high society more important than doing God's will?

Have you ever felt "used" because your obedience to a human authority caused you to miss out on a good time? This often happens when a youth obeys a parent, a wife submits to a husband, a husband sacrifices for his family, an employee submits to an employer, or a citizen submits to the government. Perhaps you feel even worse if you think the authority is unjust.

For example, suppose a teenager is invited to a party. Her unreasonable parents tell her she can't go. She graciously submits to her parents and, as a result, misses out on an evening of fun. How should she feel? Great! According to the following Scripture, God is going to make it up to her.

After saying, "Submit yourselves to every ordinance of man for the Lord's sake" (I Peter 2:13), Peter makes it clear that we are to submit "not only to the good and gentle, but also to the froward" (I Peter 2:18b), or to people who are unreasonable.

> For this is thankworthy, if a man for conscience toward God endure grief, suffering wrongfully. For what glory is it, if, when ye be buffeted for your faults, ye shall take it patiently? but, if when ye do well, and suffer for it, ye take it patiently, this is acceptable with God (I Peter 2:19-20).

We all need to examine our attitude toward submission. How do you wives react to submitting to your husbands? How do we men react when our personal desires must be put aside in order to submit to the best interest of the family?

Peter continues in the fourth chapter, verses 12-13 as follows:

> Beloved, think it not strange concerning the fiery trial which is to try you, as though some strange thing happened unto you: But rejoice, inasmuch as ye are partakers of Christ's sufferings; that, when his glory shall be revealed, ye may be glad also with exceeding joy.

Let us again consider the example of a man offered a hundred dollars tomorrow in exchange for a dollar today. Would he pout, sulk, feel sorry for himself as he gave up the dollar? Not if he had faith. He would be exuberant! Perhaps he would say, "Can I give you five? Will you take ten?" How do we react when we suffer loss for Christ? It depends on whether we have the faith which is the substance or assurance, of things hoped for, the evidence of things not seen (Hebrews 11:1). This faith makes the promises of God as real as what we can see.

2. Rewards or Treasures for Good Deeds and Sacrificial Service

In addition to rewards for losses or persecution, there are rewards for service to others. Jesus considered heavenly treasures much more valuable and, therefore, said:

> Lay not up for yourselves treasures upon earth, where moth and rust doth corrupt, and where thieves break through and steal: But lay up for yourselves treasures in heaven, where neither moth nor rust doth corrupt, and where thieves do not break through nor steal: For where your treasure is, there will your heart be also (Matthew 6:19-21).

There are many types of gifts, deeds, and services which produce rewards. Here are a few:

(1) *Leading others to righteousness.* "And they that be wise shall shine as the brightness of the firmament; and they that turn many to righteousness as the stars for ever and ever" (Daniel 12:3).

(2) *Helping the needy.* "Sell that ye have, and give alms; provide yourselves bags which wax not old, a treasure in the heavens that faileth not, where no thief approacheth, neither moth corrupteth" (Luke 12:33). "He that hath pity upon the poor lendeth unto the Lord; and that which he hath given will he pay him again" (Proverbs 19:17).

(3) *Rendering Christian hospitality.* "He that receiveth a prophet in the name of a prophet shall receive a prophet's reward; and he that receiveth a righteous man in the name of a righteous man

shall receive a righteous man's reward. And whosoever shall give to drink unto one of these little ones a cup of cold water only in the name of a disciple, verily I say unto you, he shall in no wise lose his reward" (Matthew 10:41-42).

(4)*Faithfully serving earthly masters or employers as unto the Lord.* "Servants, be obedient to them that are your masters according to the flesh, with fear and trembling, in singleness of your heart, as unto Christ; Not with eyeservice, as menpleasers, but as the servants of Christ, doing the will of God from the heart; With good will doing service, as to the Lord, and not to men: Knowing that whatsoever good thing any man doeth, the same shall he receive of the Lord, whether he be bond or free" (Ephesians 6:5-8).

The Bible makes it clear that it is not the actual amount of the service or gift that counts. God considers the ability to give or the cost to the giver. For example, Jesus said the widow's mite was larger than the gifts of the rich. "For all these have of their abundance cast in unto the offerings of God: but she of her penury hath cast in all the living that she had" (Luke 21:4).

David applied this principle when Araunah offered to give him a threshing floor and oxen to sacrifice to God.

And the king said unto Araunah, Nay; but I will surely buy it of thee at a price: neither will

I offer burnt offerings unto the Lord my God of that which doth cost me nothing. So David bought the threshingfloor and the oxen for fifty shekels of silver (II Samuel 24:24).

David realized that the offering would be worthless if it cost him nothing. It's not the amount of the gift or service but the sacrifice to the giver that counts.

3. *Authority Based on Faithfulness*

In the parable of the talents (Matthew 25:14-30) and the parable of the minas (Luke 19:12-27), Jesus teaches that our authority or rule in heaven will be in proportion to our faithfulness in the little things. He speaks of one being in authority over ten cities and another over five cities (Luke 19:17-19).

Note that it is not what you accomplish, but your faithfulness that is important. For example, suppose you hire two men to move dirt. You furnish one a bulldozer and the other a shovel. We assume the first would move much more dirt than the latter. This would not necessarily mean he was more faithful.

Jesus said, "For unto whomsoever much is given, of him shall be much required: and to whom men have committed much, of him they will ask the more" (Luke 12:48b).

Remember, it is faithfulness to our particular calling that counts. If a person is called to be a

Christian wife and mother, there is no higher calling. The important thing is how faithful we are to our own calling.

I see an illustration of this in my own family. My father is 88. He has been a very active Christian layman all of his life. He taught a men's Sunday school class of well over a hundred men for years. My mother is a great woman of prayer and an active church member, but she is the kind that gets nervous when she has to answer present in the women's missionary society. She is just not a public speaker. She said once that she felt my father and I would have treasures in heaven, but she wouldn't. I told her the reason my father was able to do what he did for the Lord was because he had a wife who backed him up and supported him. She will certainly be rewarded for any good I have done. I'm glad that when I came home she was there instead of being a busybody. I had security, love, and instruction at home. I know that I am daily backed by tremendous prayer power. Though she may not get up in front of crowds, certainly she was a good mother. Being faithful to what you are called to do is what counts.

Therefore, do not be discouraged if God does not call you to a public ministry. On the other hand, do not excuse your failure to do what you can because you cannot do as much as others.

A little poem that expresses the same sentiment goes like this:

It's not what you'd do with a million
If riches should be your lot.
But what are you doing now
With the dollar and quarter you've got?

4. Greatness Based on Humility, Servant Attitude, and Obedience

Jesus said some would be great in the kingdom and others would be least (Matthew 5:19). But His standards for greatness are quite different from the usual.

Have you ever been discouraged because you are not considered great in this life? You may never be a great athlete, actor, businessman, or statesman. You can, however, be great throughout eternity. How? By having a servant attitude and by keeping and teaching the "least" commandments.

(1) *Humility and servant's attitude.* These are high on Jesus' priority list. Time after time He tried to get His disciples to completely transform their ideas of greatness. He said:

Whosoever therefore shall humble himself as this little child, the same is greatest in the kingdom of heaven (Matthew 18:4).

But he that is greatest among you shall be your servant. And whosoever shall exalt himself shall be abased; and he that shall humble himself shall be exalted (Matthew 23:11-12).

30

But they held their peace: for by the way they had disputed among themselves, who should be the greatest. And he sat down, and called the twelve, and saith unto them, If any man desire to be first, the same shall be last of all, and servant of all (Mark 9:34-35).

And there was also a strife among them, which of them should be accounted the greatest. And he said unto them, The kings of the Gentiles exercise lordship over them; and they that exercise authority upon them are called benefactors. But ye shall not be so: but he that is greatest among you, let him be as the younger; and he that is chief, as he that doth serve (Luke 22:24-26).

Whosoever therefore shall break one of these least commandments, and shall teach men so, he shall be called the least in the kingdom of heaven; but whosoever shall do and teach them, the same shall be called great in the kingdom of heaven (Matthew 5:19).

The disciples probably agreed with Jesus intellectually but didn't apply it to themselves. At the last supper they were apparently waiting for someone "beneath" them to wash their feet. Perhaps they got the message when Jesus did this lowly job Himself.

One reason humility is so important to Jesus is that its absence caused the most traumatic experience ever to take place in heaven.

Remember that pride was the sin that caused the devil to fall (I Timothy 3:6). Satan's desire to be exalted apparently caused the original rebellion in heaven for which he was thrown out. In contrast, Christ, the supreme example of a servant attitude, was greatly exalted because, although He existed in the form of God,

> [He] thought it not robbery to be equal with God: but made himself of no reputation, and took upon him the form of a servant, and was made in the likeness of men. And being found in fashion as a man, he humbled himself, and became obedient unto death, even the death of the cross.
>
> Wherefore God also hath highly exalted him, and given him a name which is above every name. That at the name of Jesus every knee should bow, of things in heaven, and things in earth, and things under the earth; and that every tongue should confess that Jesus Christ is Lord, to the glory of God the Father (Philippians 2:6-11).

(2) *Keeping and teaching the least commandments*. In the Sermon on the Mount, Jesus said some would be called least and some would be called great in the kingdom of heaven (Matthew 5:19). Jesus gave two tests to enable you to determine which group you will be in. First, do you keep the least commandments yourself? Second, do you teach others to do so?

Why does Jesus also specify that obedience to the least commandments is important (Matthew 5:19)? Obviously, if we continue to disobey the big commandments, we won't be in heaven at all. Although we are not saved by obeying the commandments, we are saved by a faith which leads us to want to obey the Author of those commandments.

It is obedience to the least commandments—the things we often consider petty, unimportant, or picky—that determines greatness. This degree of obedience is proof of a deeper faith in God. And remember, not only is obedience to these commandments important, but also, teaching them to others.

5. *Place of Honor Based on Purity*

There are apparently special tasks in heaven reserved for those who have kept themselves pure and free from contaminating influences. Paul compares people to vessels in the following passage:

> But in a great house there are not only vessels of gold and of silver, but also of wood and of earth; and some to honour, and some to dishonour. If a man therefore purge himself from these, he shall be a vessel unto honour, sanctified, and meet for the master's use, and prepared unto every good work. Flee also youthful lusts: but follow righteousness, faith, charity, peace, with

them that call on the Lord out of a pure heart (II
Timothy 2:20-22).

Specifically, we are to stay away from anything
which causes evil, unclean, or lustful thoughts.
Some Christians excuse their watching dirty mov-
ies or reading dirty books by saying they want to
know what others are thinking. But the Bible says
God wants you to be wise in what is good, but
innocent concerning that which is evil (Romans
16:19b).

It may be possible for a man to earn some
rewards, treasures, and greatness but still be disqualified from certain honorable positions. This is
illustrated in the life of David who was permitted
to do great things for God but was forbidden to
build the temple because he had shed blood and
was a man of war (I Chronicles 28:2-3).

6. *Mercy Received Based on Mercy Given*

Jesus left no doubt that the mercy we receive
will be in proportion to the mercy we show others.
The only petition in the Lord's Prayer that Jesus
commented on further dealt with forgiving others.

And forgive us our debts, as we forgive our
debtors. For if ye forgive men their trespasses,
your heavenly Father will also forgive you: But
if ye forgive not men their trespasses, neither
will your Father forgive your trespasses (Matthew 6:12, 14-15).

One of the Beatitudes is, "Blessed are the merciful: for they shall obtain mercy" (Matthew 5:7). James said quite bluntly, "For he shall have judgment without mercy, that hath shewed no mercy; and mercy rejoiceth against judgment" (James 2:13).

In Luke 6:35, Jesus promised a great reward to those who love their enemies and who lend without expecting anything back.

In addition to the above Scriptures, Jesus makes His feelings about forgiveness plain in the parable of the unmerciful servant (Matthew 18:21-35).

Are you happy over the thought that the mercy you receive will be in proportion to the mercy you show others? If not, you have the opportunity to make the necessary changes now.

All Works Tested

We have now discussed six categories of differences in heaven which result from our earthly works. But, it is important to realize that our works will be tested by God and only those works which stand up under His test will be rewarded. Paul said:

> Every man's work shall be made manifest: for the day shall declare it, because it shall be revealed by fire; and the fire shall try every man's work of what sort it is. If any man's work abide which he hath built thereupon, he shall receive a reward (I Corinthians 3:13-15).

35

Two people who do exactly the same thing may not receive the same reward. Opportunity and motive will be considered. It is of utmost importance that our actions stem from faith, hope, and love. (This will be discussed further in Chapter 6.)

An example of the difference in God's judgment and man's is found in the parable of the laborers in the vineyard (Matthew 20:1-16). Some laborers worked all day and some worked only an hour. They all received the same pay. The point of this story is not that we will all get the same pay in heaven. This is contradicted in the preceding chapter (Matthew 19:29). The point is that if we get what is coming to us (and we will), we have no right to criticize God if He chooses to give someone else, who was not called as soon as we were, the same reward.

Note that Jesus emphasizes in Matthew 10:6-7 that the reason the last men worked only an hour was because no one hired them earlier. They were faithful from the time of their call.

Perhaps God even now is calling you to a higher level of commitment. You can be faithful to this calling by responding as Paul did:

Forgetting those things which are behind, and reaching forth unto those things which are before, I press toward the mark for the prize of the high calling of God in Christ Jesus (Philippians 3:13b-14).

Remember the foolish game show contestant at the beginning of this chapter? Jesus told the following story about a man God called a fool:

> And he spake a parable unto them, saying, The ground of a certain rich man brought forth plentifully: and he thought within himself, saying, What shall I do, because I have no room where to bestow my fruits?
>
> And he said, This will I do: I will pull down my barns, and build greater; and there will I bestow all my fruits and my goods. And I will say to my soul, Soul, thou has much goods laid up for many years; take thine ease, eat, drink, and be merry.
>
> But God said unto him, Thou fool, this night thy soul shall be required of thee: then whose shall those things be, which thou hast provided? So is he that layeth up treasure for himself, and is not rich toward God (Luke 12:16-21).

When you stand before Jesus, what will He say?
"Well done, good and faithful servant"
or
"Thou fool!"

2
Objections,
Questions,
Paradoxes

When rewards in heaven are discussed, several problems usually come to mind. As we consider rewards in heaven we will use earthly analogies to illustrate them. But remember that any physical example is only a mere hint at the infinitely greater spiritual reality.

Explaining apparent paradoxes in the Biblical teaching on heaven is like trying to explain the paradox in the theory of relativity to a two-year-old. No, we can't expect to completely understand heavenly things while in the flesh, but perhaps we can understand enough to make a difference in the way we think and live.

Some of the questions are:

(1) How does the concept of accountability for our work fit in with the concept of total forgiveness and a clean slate?

(2) If everyone is perfect in heaven, how can there be differences?

(3) How can we be happy in heaven if we are eternally conscious of the results of a wasted life?

(4) Will we be jealous there?

(5) Why did God put us on earth anyway? Why didn't He give us our spiritual bodies and put us in heaven to start with?

(6) Are heavenly considerations worthy motives?

Answers from the Scriptures

1. *Total Accountability—Total Forgiveness*

At this point, you may be wondering how the Scriptures which teach total accountability in heaven fit with the Scriptures which teach total forgiveness. Let's look at some of the Scriptures in question.

(1) *Scriptures on total accountability.*

So then every one of us shall give account of himself to God (Romans 14:12).

And whatsoever ye do, do it heartily, as to the Lord, and not unto men; Knowing that of the Lord ye shall receive the reward of the inheritance: for ye serve the Lord Christ. But he that doeth wrong shall receive for the wrong which he hath done: and there is no respect of persons (Colossians 3:23-25).

(2) *Scriptures on total forgiveness.*

I, even I, am he that blotteth out thy transgressions for mine own sake, and will not remember thy sins (Isaiah 43:25).

As far as the east is from the west, so far hath he removed our transgressions from us (Psalm 103:12).

For I will be merciful to their unrighteousness, and their sins and their iniquities will I remember no more (Hebrews 8:12).

If we confess our sins, he is faithful and just to forgive us our sins, and to cleanse us from all unrighteousness (I John 1:9).

(3) *A paradox, but no contradiction.*
The Bible teaches both total accountability and total forgiveness. Our actions have eternal consequences but our sins will be remembered no more. This is a paradox. A careful analysis, however, will show that there are three different principles involved and there is no contradiction.

First, accountability and pardon go together. Events in the life of former President Nixon and the days of the Watergate investigations helped me to understand several aspects of accountability and pardon. The Nixon tapes, for example, illustrate what Jesus meant when He said that "every idle word that men shall speak, they shall give account thereof in the day of judgment" (Matthew 12:36). Would Nixon have said what he did and used the language he used if he had known the tapes would be made public, and that he would have to account for every idle word before a much higher court than any this country can put together? Would we say what we do in the way that we do if we really believed we would have to give account someday?

But how does this fit in with the teaching of God's forgiveness and remembering our sins no more? Maybe it will be helpful to imagine a scene.

The day has come when we as Christians appear before the judgment seat of Christ. The Apostle Paul describes it in II Corinthians 5:

> For we know that if our earthly house of this tabernacle were dissolved [that is, we die] we have a building of God, an house not made with hands, eternal in the heavens (II Corinthians 5:1).
> Wherefore we labour, that ... we may be accepted of him. For we must all appear before the judgment seat of Christ; that every one may receive the things done in his body, according to that he hath done, whether it be good or bad. Knowing therefore the terror of the Lord, we persuade men; but we are made manifest unto God; and I trust also are made manifest in your consciences (II Corinthians 5:9-11).

Think of that day, standing before Jesus Christ to give an account of our lives as Christians, that we may be accepted of Him! We will already have been accepted *in* Christ (Ephesians 6:1) when we received Him as Saviour and our sins were forgiven. Now He will examine our works that we may be accepted *of* Him and He will reward us accordingly.

We approach, full of our pride. We are thinking of all the good deeds we have done and the religious services we have participated in. We are looking forward to big rewards. Just then, perhaps something like a "recorder" goes on. Every idle word comes back.

"Account for this. Account for that. Why did you talk that way? Why did you miss those opportunities to witness for Christ?"

We are thoroughly ashamed, conscience-stricken, and filled with guilt. We came expecting great rewards and now we realize we don't even deserve to get into heaven at all.

I suppose that you may be a lot like me. We know we are sinners—but frankly, we don't feel we are quite as bad as a lot of people. After all, we go to church more than most, and we don't do a lot of the bad things others do.

But I know that when I stand before the Saviour, I will realize what a terrible sinner I really am. I will appreciate more than ever what Jesus did for me! With this in mind, I want to try to see that what I do for Him now while I'm living on earth is for His glory.

The Bible says our work will be tried by fire to see "of what sort it is" (I Corinthians 3:13). If we have been building our lives with materials like wood, hay and stubble, our work will be worthless and will burn up. If it is worthwhile, it will endure.

45

If any man's work abide which he hath built thereupon, he shall receive a reward. If any man's work shall be burned, he shall suffer loss: but he himself shall be saved; yet so as by fire (verses 14, 15).

It is a solemn thought that there are eternal implications in our everyday actions as Christians. Is there something we can do now to be ready for that day? Yes, we can judge ourselves now, judge "of what sort" our work as servants of the Lord is. We can ask ourselves, "Am I doing this for Christ's sake? Will it be worthy of Him?" For, "If we would judge ourselves, we should not be judged" (I Corinthians 11:31).

As we judge ourselves, the Holy Spirit will bring to our minds those sins of omission as well as commission, and we should acknowledge our guilt (accountability), and apply God's gracious remedy for the Christian's sin: "If we confess our sins, he is faithful and just to forgive us our sins, and to cleanse us from all unrighteousness" (I John 1:9). But notice the next verse, which is also written to Christians:

If we say that we have not sinned, we make him a liar, and his word is not in us (I John 1:10).

Those sins that have been confessed to God and therefore forgiven, will not come forth to

46

accuse us when we stand before the judgment seat of Christ.

Returning to the Watergate incident, we note that much of the negative reaction to the Nixon pardon resulted from the fact that there was no accountability before the pardon. Many who believed the pardon was in the best interest of the country were disappointed because Nixon never accepted his guilt or admitted that he had done anything wrong. If he had made a full confession accompanied by repentance and remorse, there would doubtless have been much less criticism.

We can never appreciate the wonder of our complete pardon until we accept our full accountability. The two concepts are not contradictory but complementary. We will acknowledge our sins, then receive full pardon.

Second, being forgiven doesn't compensate for the consequences of a wasted life. When I was a child, my parents encouraged me to take music lessons. But practicing wasn't much fun for me. I quit. My parents do not continue to hold this over my head. I am completely forgiven.

They do not remember my failure to practice anymore. But I still cannot play the piano. If we have a family reunion and someone is needed to play the piano, no one calls on me. My parents' forgiveness didn't make up for my lack of practice.

Paul tells us that training or disciplining ourselves toward godliness will help us not only in this life, but in the life to come (I Timothy 4:7b,8). Although forgiveness is complete, it does not make up for the failure to train for godliness in this life.

Failure to lay up treasures in heaven also has nothing to do with forgiveness. Suppose I gambled and lost all our savings. My wife might completely forgive me but this would not put the money back in my bank account. The prodigal son was completely forgiven and restored as a member of the family. His pardon did not, however, restore the squandered fortune. We see then that forgiveness will not overcome the consequences of a wasted life. We are not told what the treasures are, but Jesus would not have told us to "lay up for yourselves treasures in heaven" (Matthew 6:20) if it were not possible to do so.

Third, grace, mercy and justice are compatible. People often say, "I don't want justice, I want mercy." But God can no more be unjust than He can be unmerciful. Both are a part of His nature. But how can He be both? Aren't they contradictory?

No, to the contrary, they are completely compatible. To define our terms very simply, we can think of grace as getting what we don't deserve, of mercy as not getting what we do deserve, and of justice as being treated fairly. These three concepts can be complementary.

Suppose John and Bill deserve to go to hell (as we all do). John deserves 5 stripes in hell and

Bill deserves 10. Both receive Christ, their sins are forgiven, and they get to heaven. John gets 20 rewards and Bill gets 10.

God's mercy saved each from the deserved hell. God's grace gave each infinitely more than he deserved. God's justice dealt fairly with each on an individual basis. This is no doubt oversimplified, but if I can think this up, surely God can come up with something better.

Of course, the reason God can continue to be just while justifying sinners is because of Christ Jesus who satisified His holiness.

> Whom God hath set forth to be a propitiation through faith in his blood, to declare his righteousness for the remission of sins that are past, through the forbearance of God; to declare, I say, at this time his righteousness: that he might be just, and the justifier of him which believeth in Jesus (Romans 3:25-26).

God's justice will be infinitely superior to anything we can imagine. The following Scripture teaches that God not only knows what we do and think, He knows what we would have done if we had been in different circumstances. He will judge us accordingly, as He has in every instance. Consider His judgment upon the cities and their inhabitants which were privileged to witness much of Christ's ministry.

Woe unto thee, Chorazin! woe unto thee, Bethsaida! for if the mighty works, which were done in you, had been done in Tyre and Sidon, they would have repented long ago in sackcloth and ashes. But I say unto you, It shall be more tolerable for Tyre and Sidon at the day of judgment, than for you. And thou, Capernaum, which art exalted unto heaven, shalt be brought down to hell: for if the mighty works, which have been done in thee, had been done in Sodom, it would have remained until this day. But I say unto you, That it shall be more tolerable for the land of Sodom in the day of judgment, than for thee (Matthew 11:21-24).

Remember, man looks on the outside but God looks on the heart. For this reason, we would be ill-advised to try to second-guess God.

2. *If Perfect, How Can We Be Different?*

Perfection does not mean sameness. While most believe that people and things on this earth cannot be really perfect, assume with me for a moment that they are. A perfect one-carat diamond would be different from a perfect five-carat diamond. A perfect two-seat airplane would be different from a perfect jumbo jet. A perfect water boy would be different from a perfect halfback. The perfection of heaven will not preclude differences in rewards, functions, position, or achievement.

3. *How Can We Be Happy if Conscious of a Wasted Life?*

It is true that we will not have the kind of sorrow and grief that we often experience in this life. The Bible says:

> And God shall wipe away all tears from their eyes; and there shall be no more death, neither sorrow, nor crying, neither shall there be any more pain: for the former things are passed away (Revelation 21:4).

Remember, however, that the same Bible also teaches that grief is experienced by God, the Father ("And it repented the Lord ... and it grieved him at his heart," Genesis 6:6); God, the Son ("... being grieved for the hardness of their hearts," Mark 3:5); and God, the Holy Spirit ("And grieve not the holy Spirit of God ..." Ephesians 4:30). Regardless of the theological terms we use to describe these feelings, we can't get around the fact that the Bible speaks of God as having some attitudes which can best be described by our word "grief." If God can have regrets in heaven, so can we.

But isn't this a contradiction? No. Perhaps it is a matter of degrees of sorrow or different kinds of regret. The following example, which you have probably experienced many times, might help.

A family on vacation at the beach was having a wonderful time. The father and children were

51

building a sand castle. The mother said, "I'm sorry I didn't bring my camera." Did she mean that her basic state of mind could best be characterized by the word "sorry"? Of course not. She was wonderfully happy. Her sorrow over not having something that would make a joyful occasion even better did not destroy her happiness.

Heaven will be an extremely happy place. The regrets we have for things that would make it even better will not prevent us from being joyful.

4. *Will We Be Jealous in Heaven?*

Since jealousy is listed as one of the works of the flesh (Galatians 5:20), we can be certain we won't experience it in heaven. Of course, we are talking about sinful jealousy and not the kind attributed to God in Exodus 20:5, when He said, "Thou shalt not bow down thyself to them, nor serve them: for I the Lord thy God am a jealous God, visiting the iniquity of the fathers upon the children unto the third and fourth generation of them that hate me."

George dropped out of college to get married. He always regretted that he did not finish and was envious of those who were promoted over him simply because they had a degree. However, when his own son graduated and got a good job, George rejoiced. Love for his son made the difference.

In heaven, we will have love for all and look upon each person as a member of our own family. We will rejoice at their good fortune.

5. *Why Life on Earth Anyway?*

If God wants us to live in heaven with Him and be a part of His family (and He does), why did He put us on earth to start with?

To help clarify the purpose of our present existence, suppose you had a great and wonderful task to perform. In order to accomplish your task, you built a fleet of spaceships with enormous power. They traveled at the speed of light. They were equipped with devices having unlimited capability for good or evil. They were indestructible.

Who would you choose to operate these ships? Just anybody that decided he would like to take a ride? Of course not. Some might use the enormous power you entrusted them with to hinder rather than to help you accomplish your purpose. We can be sure you would not choose anyone you could not trust completely. But how would you know who you could trust? Probably you would test your prospects thoroughly.

Perhaps you would give each prospect a temporary practice ship with limited powers. You would provide an instruction manual for the operation of the ship. You would outline the purposes for which the ship was to be used. You would expect each pilot to have his radio tuned for constant communication with you.

Then in order to test the pilot's loyalty, you would let him see that many people were doing things differently from you. If he chose to follow them instead of you, he would be disqualified immediately, and of course, you couldn't use him at all if he changed his radio to another frequency and didn't stay tuned to you for further communication and guidance.

Or suppose a prospect said, "I'll do your work, but I'm going to do it my way." Another pilot may have intended to do it your way, but he didn't spend enough time studying the instruction manual to know what your way was. And what if he polluted every place he took the ship? What about the one who used the ship for his own pleasure and forgot all about your business? Would you trust these prospects with your super ship?

Suppose your spaceship was going on a six-month journey and would need a large crew. Crew members would have to respect whatever chain of command you set up. You would devise tests of obedience under trying circumstances.

Living together in close quarters for six months, crew members would have to be able to get along with each other. You would look for qualities which would make for harmonious personal relationships—love, joy, peace, patience, kindness, goodness, faith, humility, and self-control.

What you would really be looking for is faith. If they trusted you enough to do things your way, you could trust them with your super ship. But if they put their faith in themselves or in others, they would not be chosen.

To some extent, this illustrates what God is doing with man. God has given us temporary bodies. He has assigned us a job to do and given us an instruction manual for using our temporary bodies. If we trust Him, He can trust us with the new super bodies He has designed for His heavenly family.

These two bodies are contrasted in I Corinthians 15:42-44. Here we find that there are natural bodies and spiritual bodies.

I Corinthians 15

Verse	Natural Body	Spiritual Body
42	It is sown a perishable body.	It is raised an imperishable body.
43	It is sown in dishonor.	It is raised in glory.
	It is sown in weakness.	It is raised in power.
44	It is sown a natural body.	It is raised a spiritual body.
	If there is a natural body.	There is also a spiritual body.

The natural bodies are corrupt, weak, and will

55

soon perish. The spiritual bodies are permanent and full of glory and power.

Our new bodies will be like the heavenly body of Jesus; "And as we have borne the image of the earthy, we shall also bear the image of the heavenly" (I Corinthians 15:49); "Who shall change our vile body, that it may be fashioned like unto his glorious body, according to the working whereby he is able even to subdue all things unto himself" (Philippians 3:21).

The management of the universe is to be a family affair! Those who trust God become His sons! Sons of God, not puppets or robots, not servants or slaves, but sons like Jesus! This does not mean we will be equal to Jesus. When we get to heaven we will appreciate the superiority of Jesus even more than we do now. But the Bible does say we will be like Him.

Why didn't God make us like Christ to start with? Why the necessity for the temporary body? To understand this we need to go back to that traumatic event in heaven, the rebellion and fall of Satan and his angels.

Satan, or Lucifer as he is called in Isaiah 14:12-14, along with the other angels, had a free will. Count the "I wills" there—five in two verses. He chose to rebel against God, and Jesus said in Luke 10:18 that He saw Satan fall from heaven like lightning. He and his followers were cast out.

Now, how would you like to spend eternity in heaven if every few thousand years another rebellion like that broke out? Well, don't worry. It won't happen again. Why? The earth is God's answer.

God is using earth much like the marines use boot camp or like an athletic team uses training camp. In both cases, the leaders have at least four goals:

(1) To weed out those who are not suitable.

(2) To determine in what capacity each person can best serve.

(3) To increase ability through training and practice.

(4) To learn to work together on a team, responding to the leader.

These will be discussed in detail in the next chapter.

It seems logical that God should choose to give us short—lived bodies with limited abilities for this temporary testing period on earth. Imagine the horror of an almighty, never-dying Hitler. We can't even begin to grasp the enormity of the atrocious acts he committed in a few short years. Life on earth would be impossible if the evil in men was not restrained by their weak, temporary bodies.

We may wonder why God treats us differently from the way He treated angels. We are given temporary bodies and tested before we receive our permanent bodies and go to heaven. The angels, in contrast, apparently received their permanent bodies and were placed in heaven at their creation. Why?

Angels, though so powerful that one angel could destroy 185,000 Assyrians in one night (II Kings 19:35), are not as powerful as we will be when we become like Jesus. Angels who rebel against God are capable of being bound (Revelation 20:1-3). A prison has been prepared for them from which they can never escape (Matthew 25:41). Not even hell, however, would hold us when we become like Jesus.

The new world will be controlled by Christ and Christians who, though lower than the angels for awhile, are then to be above the angels (Hebrews 2:5-17). In fact, we will judge the angels (I Corinthians 6:3). The angels are an intermediate step, sent to minister to us who shall be heirs of salvation (Hebrews 1:14). We are to reign forever (Revelation 22:5).

Earth, then, is a place for making the great decision. We can neglect that great salvation God has provided for us, go our own way, and spend eternity with all the other foolish people who choose not to trust Him. Or we can choose to trust God, and submit to His training, discipline, and work within us which prepares us to be a part of His family in heaven forever.

Not only do we choose where we will spend eternity but we also choose the nature and quality of our existence throughout eternity. This will be discussed in the next chapter.

6. *Are Heavenly Considerations Worthy Motives?*

We have all heard many criticisms of those who would think in heavenly terms. Some are considered to be so heavenly minded they are of no earthly good. The promise of "pie in the sky by and by" sometimes seems to lessen motivation for social action now. Many people feel that the reward motive is a low form of motivation and that we should be motivated only by the higher motives such as love.

While recognizing some truth in each of these criticisms, I feel we have often been faked out by the critics. It is actually the false view of heaven that leads to complacency; that is, that all will be the same regardless of how we use our time down here. If we realize the eternal consequences of how we spend our time down here, it should lead us to more involvement, not less.

Most students of motivation believe that, after the basic physical needs are met, we are usually first motivated by fear, next by rewards, and ascend from that through several steps leading to the highest motivation. For a Christian, the highest motivation must be agape love, that unconditional, self-sacrificing love which leads us to consider the objects of our love to be infinitely precious and to desire the best for them.

Motivation Seen in Scripture

To perform always on the basis of the highest level of motivation would be ideal. In practice, however, we know we do not consistently do this. The Bible, dealing with men as they are, uses all levels of motivation. Both the examples of the saints and the explicit teachings of the Scripture bring this out. We will examine first some examples and then study the specific teachings.

1. *Examples of Motivation*

Paul was motivated by so much love that he could say, "For I could wish that myself were accursed from [separated from] Christ for my brethren, my kinsmen according to the flesh" (Romans 9:3). In other words, he was willing to go to hell, if necessary, that others might be saved. But Paul was also conscious of lower motives. He was conscious of the judgment that would come if he did not serve. He said, "Woe is unto me, if I preach not the gospel!" (I Corinthians 9:16). In II Corinthians 5:10-11, he states that it is because he will appear before the judgment seat of Christ and knowing the fear of the Lord that he persuades men.

Paul was also very conscious of rewards in heaven. He said, "If in this life only we have hope in Christ, we are of all men most miserable" (I

Corinthians 15:19). He was looking forward to the crown of righteousness (II Timothy 4:8). In I Corinthians 9:24-27, Paul compares life with an athletic event. Whereas an athlete trains and disciplines himself to win a perishable wreath, Paul said we Christians do so to win an imperishable one.

Among Paul's higher motives was his response to the grace of God (I Corinthians 15:10) which will be discussed later.

Moses was also motivated on several levels. He told God, "yet now, if thou wilt forgive their sin—; and if not, blot me, I pray thee, out of thy book which thou hast written" (Exodus 32:32). Apparently, at that moment, his concern for his people was stronger than his desire for heaven. But he was also motivated by rewards. Why was he willing to give up all the privileges of being the son of Pharaoh's daughter and chose instead to endure ill treatment with the people of God? The Bible said he was looking to the reward (Hebrews 11:24-26).

Abraham also made tremendous sacrifices because he was looking for the city which has foundations, whose architect and builder is God (Hebrews 11:10).

Other heroes of faith "were tortured, not accepting deliverance; that they might obtain a better resurrection" (Hebrews 11:35b).

Even Jesus endured the cross for the joy that was set before Him (Hebrews 12:2).

What was this joy set before Him? We assume it was the joy of having us as part of His family forever. Just think, He gets us and we get Him. Who do you think gets the better end of this deal? If He was willing to sacrifice so much, with us as the reward, how much more should we be willing to sacrifice to get Him!

Modern day saints have also had a view of eternity. Missionary Jim Elliot, who was martyred by the Auca Indians, wrote sometime earlier, "He is no fool who gives what he cannot keep, to gain what he cannot lose."

I am certain that all of us, if we carefully examine our own motives, would find various levels of motivation. It appears that, in my own experience, the big decisions and issues of life are decided on higher motivations while some of the day-to-day transactions are brought about by lower motivations. I like to think, for example, that the motive for my overall commitment to study the Bible is of a high type. However, on a particular Tuesday night I might take the trouble to memorize a verse of Scripture our Bible study group had agreed to memorize because I would be ashamed in front of my friends if I did not know it.

At the age of thirty-three, I decided to give up a very lucrative secular business in order to give more time to the Lord's work. This eventually led to my ministry at Look-Up Lodge retreat center. While I had very high motives for making this

original commitment, my going out on a particular Saturday evening when I am exhausted
may arise more from a sense of duty or the
consequences to my ministry if I do not go.

2. *Specific Teachings of Motivation*
The Bible has a great deal to say about motivation on many different levels. In *Nave's Topical
Bible,* which lists Scriptures under varying headings, there are seven-and-a-half columns of small
print under the heading, "Fear, a motive for obedience." There are six columns under the heading, "Rewards, a motive for obedience."
Jesus certainly used all levels. He used fear in
such passages as Luke 12:4-5:

> And I say unto you my friends, Be not afraid
> of them that kill the body, and after that have
> no more that they can do. But I will forewarn
> you whom ye shall fear: Fear him, which after
> he hath killed hath power to cast into hell; yea,
> I say unto you, Fear him.

Note that fear in this sense is not just reverence but actual fear of the consequences.
Among the many passages which indicate that
Jesus used motivation by rewards is Matthew
19:21 where He used the promise of reward to
motivate giving to the poor:

> Jesus said unto him, If thou wilt be perfect,
> go and sell that thou hast, and give to the poor,

and thou shalt have treasure in heaven: and come and follow me.

Paul also often used this method to produce action and spiritual growth in his hearers, such as when he wrote to the saints in Colosse:

If ye then be risen with Christ, seek those things which are above, where Christ sitteth on the right hand of God. Set your affection on things above, not on things on the earth. For ye are dead, and your life is hid with Christ in God. When Christ, who is our life, shall appear, then shall ye also appear with him in glory. (Colossians 3:1-4).

Chapter 1 of this book also contains additional quotes from both Jesus and Paul.

Peter wrote that belief in the return of Jesus should motivate us to holy living (II Peter 3:11-14). Much of the Revelation contains promises to him who overcomes.

Heretofore we have been speaking of rewards as a lower motivation. However, if we think of love as the highest motivation, the concept of rewards would also fit in nicely. Jesus said that the greatest commandment was to love God and the second greatest was to love our neighbor as ourselves (Matthew 22:36-39). We are taught, then, that we should love God first, then others as ourselves.

How would the concept of rewards fit in with our love for God? When we love someone, we want to please them. Much of my early motivation was to please my parents. When I made wise choices, my parents beamed. Since God loves us more than human parents ever could, we know it pleases Him when we make wise choices. We also know we can grieve the Holy Spirit (Ephesians 4:30) by acting unwisely.

Imagine this scene. A couple works and sacrifices so their son can go to college. He graduates with honors and attains a position with great opportunity. How happy the parents would be to know that their sacrifices were not in vain! Love for his parents and a desire to please them would be strong motivation for the young student.

Paul seemed to have a similar motive for serving God when he said:

> But by the grace of God I am what I am: and His grace which was bestowed upon me was not in vain; but I laboured more abundantly than they all: yet not I, but the grace of God which was with me (I Corinthians 15:10).

Realizing that he could have done nothing except for the grace of God, Paul was anxious that this grace not be in vain. He therefore labored diligently.

In numerous places in the Bible the Christian's reward is referred to as a crown. For example Paul states:

Henceforth there is laid up for me a crown of righteousness, which the Lord, the righteous judge, shall give me at that day: and not to me only, but unto all them also that love his appearing (II Timothy 4:8).

In Revelation 4:10 we are told that believers in heaven will "cast their crowns before the throne, saying, Thou art worthy, O Lord, to receive glory and honour, and power: for thou hast created all things, and for thy pleasure they are and were created."

We should all be looking forward to the day when we can lay our crowns before the Lord Jesus Christ. Our love for Him should lead us to want more crowns or rewards to cast at His feet. Granted, not many people will be motivated on this high a level. The point is, however, that regardless of the level of motivation, it should stem from an eternal perspective.

This eternal view will help us see things as God does, especially when defining true love. For instance, if we truly love our neighbor we will also want the very best for him. We know that every Christian person will stand before the judgment seat of Christ and that his eternal welfare will depend on decisions made in this life. Therefore, if we really love, we will try our best to help them prepare for eternity. It is obvious that if we love ourselves in the right way, we will also wish to prepare ourselves for eternity.

In summary, considering life from the eternal viewpoint is a worthy motivation. It can appeal to lower motivations as this is where many people are. However, it can also appeal to the very highest motivations; it is Biblical, and has greatly influenced the lives of the saints.

3
Earth—
Training Camp
for Heaven

The coach's voice rang out: "Sanders at right end. Finch at right tackle . . . Hart at halfback." Hart's heart leaped for joy. He had made the team. The weeks of working to the point of exhaustion, the aching muscles, the bruises had paid off. At least four things had happened.

(1) The coaches had decided who would be on the team and who wouldn't. Hart was accepted.

(2) Those who had made the team were assigned positions. Hart would play halfback.

(3) Hart's effectiveness had increased through training and practice.

(4) Hart had learned to work together as a team with the other chosen men, responding to the instructions of the coach.

Servicemen go through a similar experience in basic training. Some are eliminated entirely. Those who remain are tested to determine the kind of duty they are best suited for. They are trained to function better. And individuals are taught to work as a team and to respond to the chain of command.

We may think of earth as a training camp for heaven where the same four things are accomplished. The first two were mainly covered earlier and will only be briefly mentioned here to keep them in perspective. The last two will be the primary emphasis of this chapter.

Selection of God's Team

God separates all men into two groups as a shepherd separates the sheep from the goats. The chosen go to the kingdom prepared from the creation of the world and the rest to the eternal fire prepared for the devil and his angels (Matthew 25:31-46).

The basis of the choice is grace on God's part and faith on our part. Since faith is so fundamental in all of the above, we will be considering it in a separate chapter.

Determining Our Position

Second, God determines what our position in heaven will be. Some of the criteria for this choice were given in chapter one. The way we train and prepare ourselves will also be a factor, as we will see under the next heading.

Training for Heaven

Third, earth is used as a place to train ourselves to be the best possible members of God's team. This is where so many Christians fail. How many people in your church train as hard to be a better Christian as guys on a football team do to be a better football player? Yet, Paul said spiritual training is much more important (I Timothy 4:7-8).

According to Paul, there are two times when we benefit from godly training. The rest of the time, it doesn't make any difference. When are the two times? See if you can find them in the following passages:

Exercise [train] thyself rather unto godliness. For bodily exercise [physical training] profiteth little: but godliness is profitable unto all things, having promise of the life that now is, and of that which is to come (I Timothy 4:7b-8).

Paul compares spiritual training with bodily training or discipline. He says the two times when spiritual training benefits us are in this life and in the life to come. Other than these two times, it makes no difference, which is to say that spiritual training is always desirable. Much has been written on how a godly life is the most meaningful, fulfilling life possible in the here and now. But note that spiritual training also benefits us in the life to come. We are not told how the training we receive in this life will carry forward to the next, but simply that training will be of value. After making this point, Paul continues:

This is a faithful saying and worthy of all acceptation. For therefore we both labour and suffer reproach, because we trust in the living God, who is the Saviour of all men, specially of those that believe. These things command and teach (I Timothy 4:9-11).

73

Note that this teaching motivated Paul to labor and strive.

Paul also compares physical training with spiritual training in I Corinthians 9:24-27:

> Know ye not that they which run in a race run all, but one receiveth the prize? So run, that ye may obtain. And every man that striveth for the mastery is temperate in all things. Now they do it to obtain a corruptible crown; but we an incorruptible. I therefore so run, not as uncertainly; so fight I, not as one that beateth the air: but I keep under my body, and bring it into subjection: lest that by any means, when I have preached to others, I myself should be a castaway.

Again he makes the point that spiritual training is of much greater importance than athletic training because of the eternal consequences (verse 25). Yet, most church members fail to train spiritually as diligently as athletes do physically.

Paul worked in order that he wouldn't be disqualified (a "castaway," verse 27). We know from such passages as Romans 8:16, 35-39, and II Timothy 1:12 that Paul was not concerned about losing his salvation. Paul was training so he wouldn't be disqualified for service.

Note that while Paul was conscious of training for the future, he was also aware of the importance of the race he was running now. That is, he was both "training" and "on the job." Therefore, we can think of life on earth as "on-the-job training."

Since the preceding verses speak of preaching the gospel and becoming all things to all men in order to save some, it would seem that Paul considered himself in a race against time for the hearts and minds and souls of men. If we think of men being on this earth for just an instant, and that what they do during that instant affects all eternity, we see how the sense of a race applies.

Some might wonder how we should divide our time between training for heaven and doing our job down here. There should be no conflict. The two go together. The best way we can prepare for eternity is to be faithful in our present assignments.

During training, a coach assigns exercises which he thinks will most benefit the team. Some exercises are assigned to all. Others are assigned to certain individuals based on their need and on the job they are expected to perform. For example, a tackle does not spend time practicing passing as a quarterback does.

We can be certain God has the wisdom to include in our training course just what is best for the assignment we will have in eternity. Therefore, as we prepare to do God's will effectively now, we are preparing for heaven. And remember, Jesus said, "And that servant, which knew his lord's will, and *prepared not* himself, neither did according to his will, shall be beaten with many stripes" (Luke 12:47; emphasis mine).

Since we can't imagine literal whippings in heaven, we must assume that Jesus is speaking of less rewards. This is indicated in the preceding verses which say:

> And the Lord said, Who then is that faithful and wise steward, whom his lord shall make ruler over his household, to give them their portion of meat in due season?
>
> Blessed is that servant, whom his lord when he cometh shall find so doing. Of a truth I say unto you, that he will make him ruler over all that he hath (Luke 12:42-44).

Still another illustration from racing is found in Hebrews 12:1-2:

> Wherefore seeing we also are compassed about with so great a cloud of witnesses, let us lay aside every weight, and the sin which doth so easily beset us, and let us run with patience the race that is set before us, looking unto Jesus the author and finisher of our faith; who for the joy that was set before him endured the cross, despising the shame, and is set down at the right hand of the throne of God.

We are exhorted to lay aside every weight or encumbrance and sin in order to run the race.

That is, anything that slows us down in the race set before us is wrong for us.

Hebrews 12:1 refers to the "great cloud of witnesses surrounding us." These are the heroes of faith of chapter 11 who, as we have seen, made great sacrifices in this life because they were considering the eternal consequences, as is indicated by such phrases as, "for he had respect unto the recompence of the reward" (11:26) and "that they might obtain a better resurrection" (11:35).

Because of these witnesses, we are to put aside anything, however good it might be, if it slows us down. There is a difference of opinion about whether the "cloud of witnesses" means that the heroes of faith are currently watching us run our race, or whether it means they have witnessed to us.

If we accept the former, the scene is that of a great arena in which all the saints are watching us run our particular race. Imagine that we were watching the Olympics or another race that was very important to us. How would we feel if the runner we were pulling for was distracted by events on the sidelines? Suppose he carried a little radio along with him and held it up to his ear while running. Or suppose he was just not really doing his best. We would want to say, "Run, man! Forget the sidelines! Throw away your radio! Run!"

What would be the message of the saints of the Bible, or perhaps, of our loved ones who have gone on, if they saw us running our race? Would they say, "Quit fooling around. Quit majoring on minors. Quit being distracted by things that won't make a bit of difference 1,000 years from now." Or, in Bible language, "Lay aside every weight [encumbrance], and the sin which doth so easily beset us, and let us run with patience [endurance] the race that is set before us" (Hebrews 12:1b).

If we take the "witnesses" of this passage to be those who have witnessed to us, the message is the same. Get busy about things that are of eternal significance!

An athlete would not have to do anything bad to be considered a bad player. If he failed to get involved, failed to put forth his best effort, he would be unacceptable.

In the military one of the biggest crimes is desertion. Here again, the soldier may not have been doing anything bad—he just failed to be at his place of duty.

Jesus made this point in the parable of the talents where He used the word "wicked." This is such a hard word that Jesus seldom used it in reference to humans. He used it often when referring to Satan. What awful crime was committed in order to make the loving Jesus call someone wicked? The man Jesus called wicked did not do one single thing bad. He had a talent and he buried it. The reason he buried it was the same

78

reason we bury ours—he was afraid (Matthew 25:25).

> His lord answered and said unto him, Thou wicked and slothful servant... cast ye the unprofitable servant into outer darkness: there shall be weeping and gnashing of teeth (Matthew 25:26, 30).

As in the illustration of the spaceships in Chapter 2, we would not necessarily have to do anything bad in the trial ship to fail to qualify for the super ship. A candidate would fail if he did not trust the master enough to use the trial ship for his purposes.

Sue was critically injured in an automobile accident. As she lay dying in the hospital she told her mother,"You taught me how to hold a cigarette, how to hold a cocktail glass, how to have sex without getting pregnant, but you never taught me how to die. You better teach me now because I don't have very long."

Sue and her mother, like everyone else, were put here for an instant in time to prepare themselves and others for eternity. Like most, they failed.

In the spaceship analogy, the test vehicle represented our present temporary bodies while the ultimate spaceship represented the glorified, supernatural bodies those who pass the test will receive. We stated that while in this temporary body, we not only decide where we will spend eternity, but we determine the quality of our eternal existence.

Let's now turn to examine our test vehicle, the temporary body, and see how we can best use the time we spend in it.

First, realize that man is not just a biochemical machine called a body. Instead of *being* a body, we *have* a body. This body includes a biochemical computer called a brain. In II Corinthians 5:1-10, Paul compares our body to a tent which we long to put aside in order to be clothed with our dwelling from heaven. He desired to be absent from the body and to be at home with the Lord. Paul said, "We have this treasure in earthen vessels" (II Corinthians 4:7a). Peter also wrote of laying aside his earthly dwelling (II Peter 1:13-14).

The real "I" dwells in a body which will some-day be exchanged for a new glorified body. In the meantime, our present body is the "machine" we use in our "on-the-job training."

Perhaps the eternal view could help us get a more accurate selfimage. Failure to see this present life in perspective leads some to be overly concerned about faults of the temporary body, yet leads others to think more highly of themselves than they ought (Romans 12:3).

For example, an air force pilot learning to fly in a small trainer should not be discouraged because he cannot get the level of performance a pilot in a sophisticated jet does. No one expects him to.

On the other hand, the jet pilot has no occasion for pride because he can go faster than the training plane. The key in each case is how well they perform with what they have to work with. Are they learning the lesson they were supposed to at each stage?

Some people have better bodies, better brains, better opportunities than others. This should cause no pride among the "haves" nor sorrow among the "have–nots." All Christians will get infinitely superior bodies later on. Be diligent, however, to get full benefit out of the body and opportunities God gave you.

It is not always possible for us to determine whether poor behavior is caused by a poor body or a poor spirit. Perhaps this is one reason Jesus did not assign the job of judging to us.

For example, a casual listener may not be able to determine if bad music was caused by a bad piano or by a bad piano player. He may know something was missing but not know what. A musician may know that a note was missing but would not know whether it was due to a stuck key or a poor piano player. Only by observing would he know. If it turned out to be a stuck key we would not worry so much if we were hiring the piano player. He would be getting a better piano later. Also a piano player should not feel guilty if the fault is in the piano.

We may not always know if a particular personality fault is due to a bad computer (brain) or a bad spirit. This may cause us to have false guilt over some things that are of no eternal concern. Our new glorified computer will not give us the problems this one does.

On the other hand, we may accept too lightly, excuse, or rationalize faults of the spirit. We are responsible for yielding to God's computer rather than ours when we have a choice. Also, we are responsible for reprogramming our computers. Failure in either instance does have eternal significance and should not lead us to accept our actions as "just human nature."

We must also remember that we are commanded to "be filled with the Spirit" (Ephesians 5:18) and that Jesus said the disciples would receive power when the Holy Spirit had come upon them (Acts 1:8). Since the power of the Holy Spirit is now available to all Christians, we will not be excused because we are unable to perform Christian service in our own strength. We were never meant to.

Suppose a pilot in training crashed because he ran out of gas. What kind of excuse would it be to say, "It's not my fault. You can't expect a plane to fly without gas."

His excuse would be unacceptable because one of his duties is to check the gas before taking off. he will be held accountable for failure to perform up to the level which could be attained if we followed the command to be filled with the Spirit.

People who beg to be excused from Christian service because they are untrained will face the question, Why? When classics of the faith are available in paperback for a few dollars, there is no excuse for anyone who can read not to be a well-trained servant of the Lord. There is no excuse for failure to follow the Biblical command to:

> Study to shew thyself approved unto God, a workman that needeth not to be ashamed, rightly dividing the word of truth (II Timothy 2:15).

Paul combines the military analogy with the athletic analogy in the following passage:

> Thou therefore endure hardness, as a good soldier of Jesus Christ. No man that warreth entangleth himself with the affairs of this life; that he may please him who hath chosen him to be a soldier.
>
> And if a man also strive for masteries, yet is he not crowned, except he strive lawfully.
>
> The husbandman that laboureth must be first partaker of the fruits. Consider what I say; and the Lord give thee understanding in all things (II Timothy 2:3-7).

A fighter pilot wants his plane in the best possible condition. He wants it fine tuned to get the best possible performance. The plane is stripped of all luxuries and unnecessary weight and carries only what will improve its performance or provide needed protection.

A Christian, then, takes care of his body, not only because it is the temple of God and should be kept holy (I Corinthians 3:16-17), but also because it is the vehicle we use for serving God.

Since the main contest we are engaged in is for the mind (II Corinthians 10:3-5), we are particularly conscious of keeping our brain in the best possible condition. Of course, we should eliminate anything, such as alcohol or other drugs, which would impair its performance. But we should go further than this.

Just as warplanes have stored in their computers the information considered most helpful in fulfilling their mission, so we should store in our computers (brains) the information which we need. Since about nine-tenths of what we do results from the subconscious, it is important that we reprogram our computers so that even our subconscious reactions will be correct. We do this by meditating on the Word day and night (Psalm 1:2) and by following the admonition of Philippians 4:8 which says:

Finally, brethren, whatsoever things are true, whatsoever things are honest, whatsoever things are just, whatsoever things are pure, whatsoever things are lovely, whatsoever things are of good report; if there be any virtue, and if there be any praise, think on these things.

In addition to striving to make our bodies as efficient as possible, we need to keep our job or mission clearly in focus. Our overall assignment for this life is summed up in what we call the Great Commission, Matthew 28:18-20. Here Jesus identifies Himself as the one who also rules the universe by saying, "All authority has been given to me in heaven and on earth." He then gives us our assignment, "Go ye therefore and teach [make disciples] ... baptizing ... teaching them to observe all things whatsoever I have commanded you ..."

As we become involved in the Great Commission, we see that there is no conflict between being heavenly minded and being of earthly good. From the eternal point of view, making disciples is the best possible thing we can do, both for ourselves and for those we disciple. Also, since the very best possible way to live on this earth is to live in accordance with the teachings of Jesus; observing His commandments and teaching others to do so is the best thing we can do as far as this life is concerned. The service for our fellowman, motivated by love, which will result from our following Jesus' teachings will be discussed in Chapter 6.

We see, then, that we do not have to choose between being relevant to this age and being relevant to the life to come. The two go together. As Paul said in I Timothy 4:7-8, spiritual discipline and training helps both in this life and the life to come. Not only does it benefit us, but it also benefits others.

While the Great Commission applies to all Christians, our particular function in carrying it out varies from person to person. In Romans 12 and I Corinthians 12, Paul compares the church to a body composed of many different members. Each member has its own separate function and should not complain because it cannot do what other parts of the body do. If we have a less honorable task or an inferior body, we should realize that this, in itself, is of no eternal significance. It's faithfulness with what we have that counts.

Team Work

When I entered basic training in the Air Force, the drill sergeant often told us to do things which seemed rather stupid to me. I didn't tell him so. I realized that the activity itself was not as important as our learning to obey orders.

Military men through the ages have realized that an undisciplined unit would lose battles they would otherwise have won. Many athletic teams with players of great individual ability have lost games because of lack of teamwork.

The fall of Satan was discussed in Chapter 2. The reason for his fall was that he was unwilling to be a team player. He was unwilling to let God be Lord, coach, commanding general. Self-aggrandizement was more important than the welfare of the group.

Faith in God as our commander and love for Him and for our fellowmen are characteristics that will make us good team members. These will be discussed later. But for now, recognize that knowing we should live by faith and love doesn't enable us to do so. We must practice—practice—practice.

In summary, we are put on this speck called earth for an instant in eternity to make the big decision: will we put our faith in God and spend eternity with others who put their faith in Him, or will we trust ourselves and spend eternity with others who trust themselves? If we have chosen to trust God, why do we continue to hang around on earth? Why not go on to our eternal home? We hang around for as long as God chooses to leave us here for two reasons. We devote the rest of our lives:

(1) To helping as many others as possible make the correct decision, and

(2) Training ourselves and others to be the best possible citizens of heaven.

YOUR REWARDS IN HEAVEN

Then we will be able to say with Paul:

I have fought a good fight, I have finished my course, I have kept the faith: henceforth there is laid up for me a crown of righteousness, which the Lord, the righteous judge, shall give me at that day: and not to me only, but unto all them also that love his appearing (II Timothy 4:7-8).

4
These Present Sufferings

Suffering is one of the biggest problems many people have in accepting that there is a God of love. Many atheists and agnostics take the position that there cannot be a God who is both all-powerful and all-loving because evil and pain exist. Either He cannot prevent suffering or does not wish to. They argue that if the former is true, He is not omnipotent, and if the latter is true, He is not loving.

This type of thinking results from a failure to see life on earth from God's point of view. Of course, we could never even begin to see things from God's point of view unless He chose to reveal them, as the following Scripture says:

> The secret things belong unto the Lord our God: but those things which are revealed belong unto us and to our children for ever (Deuteronomy 29:29).

Suppose that molecules of lubricant inside a watch had intelligence. Their universe would be that portion of the watch they could observe. Could they understand anything of their purpose, or of the purpose of the watch, or of the watchmaker? Would it be of any concern to them whether the watch was being used to time a horse race or a flight to the moon? If the owner of the watch wished to inform them through some form of mental telepathy, how could he do it? What words in their vocabulary would enable them to understand a horse or spaceship or moon?

Since the purpose of lubricant is to reduce friction, we assume the lubricant would be placed where the friction was the greatest. Obviously, the molecules would not be able to understand why an intelligent watchmaker would put them in such a spot. They could not be expected to know anything of ultimate meaning and purpose unless it was revealed to them.

It is almost as ridiculous to see the philosophers vainly trying to figure out what life is all about. Could an ant crawling through Space Control Laboratory in Houston figure out what it was all about? No, we can only know what God has chosen to reveal.

The fact is, however, that He has chosen to reveal some things about suffering which we will discuss under the following headings: Eternal View Necessary for Understanding, Cause of Suffering, and Response to Suffering.

Eternal View Necessary for Understanding

Imagine a virus that has a life span of three seconds. He is born in a doctor's office just as the doctor inserts a needle into a man's arm. In the virus' old age, the doctor pulls the needle out. For most of the virus' life, the patient is grimacing with pain. Would he not consider the doctor to be a cruel person? Would he not think the patient a fool to submit to the doctor without a struggle?

Suppose that what the virus did not know was that the patient had just won a six–month trip

around the world. This, of course, would be quite
meaningless to a virus whose concept of the universe would be whatever part of the doctor's office
he could see. Also, of what value would the promise
of pleasure next week be to one with a three–second life span? A week would be 201,000 life spans
or the equivalent of over 14 million years to a man
with a life span of 70 years.

The man, however, would have an entirely different view of the office visit. He would not consider the two or three seconds of pain worthy to be
compared with the fun he would have on the trip.
Paul felt the same way about our earthly life
compared to eternity. He said:

> For I reckon that the sufferings of this present
> time are not worthy to be compared with the
> glory which shall be revealed in us (Romans
> 8:18).

To get this verse in context, Paul was comparing
the sufferings of this life to the pain of childbirth.
Which is of greater concern to a parent during
childbirth—the immediate comfort of the emerg-
ing infant or his coming whole and healthy? God
sees the time spent in this life compared to eternity as infinitely less than the time spent in labor
compared to the remainder of life on earth. He is
therefore not as concerned with our comfort in this
life as He is with our development into sons of
God. That is why He could inspire James to write:

My brethren, count it all joy when ye fall into divers temptations; knowing this, that the trying of your faith worketh patience. But let patience have her perfect work, that ye may be perfect and entire, wanting nothing (James 1:2-4).

My brother's small daughter swallowed a number of aspirin and was rushed to the doctor. As the doctor pumped the child's stomach, she pleadingly looked to her father for help. Instead of rescuing her, her father helped the doctor by holding her. Most parents have had similar experiences of hurting their children or holding them while someone else hurt them. Unlike the child, the parent understands that temporary pain is sometimes necessary.

Paul expressed the temporary versus eternal as follows:

For our light affliction, which is but for a moment, worketh for us a far more exceeding and eternal weight of glory (II Corinthians 4:17).

Compared to eternity, Paul saw his affliction as momentary and light. In the same letter he described some of his afflictions:

Of the Jews five times received I forty stripes save one. Thrice was I beaten with rods, once was I stoned, thrice I suffered shipwreck, a night and a day I have been in the deep; in journeyings often, in perils of waters, in perils of robbers, in perils by mine own countrymen, in perils by the heathen, in perils in the city, in perils in the wilderness, in perils in the sea, in perils among false brethren; in weariness and painfulness, in watchings often, in hunger and thirst, in fastings often, in cold and nakedness.

Beside those things that are without, that which cometh upon me daily, the care of all the churches. Who is weak, and I am not weak? who is offended, and I burn not? (II Corinthians 11:24-29).

You can see that only with an eternal viewpoint could these afflictions be considered light.

The differences in our assessment of a situation, depending on whether we take a short term or long term view, can be illustrated by the following analogy.

Suppose Richie, son and sole heir of an unusually wealthy man, is playing Monopoly with Poorly, a penniless orphan. Poorly owns most of the property, has homes, hotels, and an ample supply of cash. Richie is on the verge of bankruptcy.

Which one would you feel sorry for? Who is better off? It would depend on your time reference. Poorly is best situated for the short term and Richie for a longer term. However, to know who is really better off, you would need to consider a different set of criteria altogether—their preparation for eternity.

We would expect Richie to be momentarily sad if he landed on Park Place and lost everything, but we would hardly expect him to commit suicide over it. If he was overly distraught, we would try to get him to see that it was only a game and had nothing to do with the "real world."

We must realize that this earth is not our real world. Accordingly, Paul wept for those "who set their minds on earthly things."

> For our conversation [citizenship] is in heaven; from whence also we look for the Saviour, the Lord Jesus Christ: Who shall change our vile body, that it may be fashioned like unto his glorious body, according to the working whereby he is able even to subdue all things unto himself (Philippians 3:19-21).

Jesus demonstrated how a different point of view can radically change our assessment of a situation in His comments about the churches at Smyrna and Laodicea. To the former, He said, "I know thy works, and tribulation, and poverty, (but thou art rich)" (Revelation 2:9). To the church at Laodicea He said, "Because thou sayest, I am rich, and increased with goods, and have need of nothing; and knowest not that thou art wretched, and miserable, and poor, and blind, and naked" (Revelation 3:17).

The world saw the church at Smyrna in the midst of tribulation and poverty, but Jesus saw them as rich. The Laodiceans thought they were rich but Jesus saw them as bankrupt. Which situation would you rather be in?

When we are tempted to doubt God's love, we must remember that it is in the ages to come, not here, that the riches of God's grace will be manifest. Paul specifically states this in the following:

> And hath raised us up together, and made us sit together in heavenly places in Christ Jesus: that *in the ages to come* he might shew the exceeding riches of his grace in his kindness toward us through Christ Jesus (Ephesians 2:6-7, emphasis mine).

It is in the ages to come, not in this life, that we will experience the fullness of God's grace.

Many parts of the Bible do not make sense unless we see them from God's point of view instead of man's. An example is found in the Book of Job.

Job 1:2-3 describes the wealth which Job had and later lost. Job 42:10 records that God restored to Job twice as much as he had before. Job 42:12-13 gives the results of this restoration. Let's check God's math:

Before (Job 1:2-3)	*After (Job 42:12-13)*
7,000 sheep	x 2 = 14,000 sheep
3,000 camels	x 2 = 6,000 camels

500 yoke of oxen	x 2 =	1,000 yoke of oxen
500 female donkeys	x 2 =	1,000 female donkeys
7 sons	x 2 =	7 sons
3 daughters	x 2 =	3 daughters

God's math agrees with ours until we get to the sons and daughters. How do we explain this? From God's point of view, the 7,000 sheep ceased to exist when they died. Fourteen thousand new sheep were required to replace them. The sons and daughters who died were more alive than ever, however. God could see them happy in heaven. Job needed a total of 14 sons and 6 daughters in order to have twice as many as before. The 7 new sons and 3 new daughters, added to the ones now in heaven, gave him this total. From God's timeless point of view, he saw the entire family united in heaven through all eternity. The brief period of separation was insignificant in comparison.

There is no evidence that God told Job that part of the promise would be fulfilled in this life and part in eternity. If Job had thought only in terms of this life he would have thought God had not kept all of His promise.

People today often think that all of God's promises for deliverance, healing, etc., will be fulfilled in this life if we have enough faith. This is not so. God sometimes gives partial fulfillment as He did in the case of Job, but most of His promises are for eternity.

Of course, those with real faith would prefer eternal fulfillment anyway. Suppose a father sells a piece of property for a large sum of money. He comes home and finds his children playing Monopoly. Each child is engrossed in trying to accumulate as much play money as possible.

The father tells them that due to a fortunate sale, he is going to give each child $10,000.00. Would they expect or want the promise fulfilled with the play money they are involved with at the moment? Of course not. They all know the game will be over shortly and success or failure in the game will have no lasting significance.

Don't be confused because many of the promises of the Bible are in the present or past tense. Time means nothing to God. God sees things in the present tense although, from our point of view, they are still future. Paul said that God calls things that are not as though they were (Romans 4:17).

In addition to considering the brevity of any suffering compared to eternity, an eternal view should also lead us to appreciate the training value of hardship.

Suppose a mother goes to watch her son practice football. She sees him and others pushing a blocking dummy along the ground with the mean old coach standing on it to make it heavier. She tells him to get off and put wheels under it to make it easier. When the coach tells the team to run laps, she gives her son a mini-bike. At first she might appear to be a loving mother, but we would know better. The coach makes practice hard for the benefit of the players and the team.

Many pilots have learned to fly with the aid of a link trainer. This trainer resembles the cockpit of an airplane but never goes anywhere. The trainer can simulate all types of flying conditions. If he really loved the trainee, what would he do? Simulate a flight which took off in perfect weather, flew along with no problems whatsoever, and landed under ideal conditions? No, he would simulate thunderstorms, instrument malfunctions, and all kinds of problems. Is this the loving thing to do? Yes, because it helps the pilot prepare.

A person who does not understand football may wonder why a coach trains a defensive tackle one way and a quarterback another way. Only God knows what place of service we will have in heaven. Therefore, only God knows the kind of training we need down here. We do not always know how suffering fits in but we can be assured that God knows. Paul said, "And not only so, but we glory in tribulations also: knowing that tribulation worketh patience; and patience, experience; and experience, hope" (Romans 5:3-4). A similar statement by James was previously quoted.

This does not mean that we purposely bring suffering upon ourselves for no reason, or that we do not act with compassion to help alleviate the suffering of others. In the section on love in Chapter 6 we will consider a number of Scriptures commanding us to relieve suffering and to promote the welfare of others in the present life. However, when suffering is unavoidable or necessary to accomplish a higher purpose, we should rejoice in it.

We may still wonder why a loving God permits suffering at all, however brief it might be compared to eternity. We therefore consider the causes of suffering in the next section.

Cause of Suffering

We will consider suffering under two headings: Suffering Directly From God and Suffering Indirectly From God.

1. *Suffering Directly From God*

Many of us have the feeling that if God were perfectly just, He would find a way to be fair to those who trust Him. We are all aware that some Christians seem to suffer so much more than others. A just God should compensate for this. The whole thesis of this book is that God will do that. He will do much more than make up for all our sufferings in heaven. Justice will be done. Those who deserve the most will get the most.

All who get to heaven get much more than they deserve, but those who deserve more will get proportionately that much more than they deserve.

A loving God may directly bring about suffering for the purpose of judgment, discipline, or training. The following passages emphasize that it is because of love that God chastens His own. The word "chasten" in the passages quoted below is translated "discipline" "punish" and "train" in other translations.

As many as I love, I rebuke and chasten: be zealous therefore, and repent (Revelation 3:19).

And ye have forgotten the exhortation which speaketh unto you as unto children, My son, despise not thou the chastening of the Lord, nor faint when thou art rebuked of him; for whom the Lord loveth, he chasteneth, and scourgeth every son whom he receiveth.

If ye endure chastening, God dealeth with you as with sons; for what son is he whom the father chasteneth not? But if ye be without chastisement, whereof all are partakers, then are ye bastards, and not sons.

Furthermore, we have had fathers of our flesh which corrected us, and we gave them reverence: shall we not much rather be in subjection unto the Father of spirits, and live? For they verily for a few days chastened us after their own pleasure; but he for our profit, that we might be partakers of his holiness.

Now no chastening for the present seemeth to be joyous, but grievous: nevertheless afterward it yieldeth the peaceable fruit of righteousness unto them which are exercised thereby (Hebrews 12:5-11).

We see that chastening is an evidence of our relationship with God. Christians often wonder why their non-Christian friends can seem to sin and get away with it. I used to wonder why some of my friends could have so much fun sinning and I couldn't. I knew the Bible said there was pleasure in sin for a season but I couldn't enjoy it even for the season. If I didn't get caught from without, I would surely get caught from within. I found the reason—God isn't going to let his own enjoy sinning.

God may also need to remove things in our lives which take time and energy away from God-given tasks. Jesus said, "Every branch in me that beareth not fruit he taketh away: and every branch that beareth fruit, he purgeth it, that it may bring forth more" fruit (John 15:2).

We have been speaking thus far about God's dealings with His own, but what about the judgment of those who are not His? Much of their present misery results from the fallen world and will be dealt with in the next chapter. Of course, the greatest judgment will be in the life to come, and this will also be dealt with in the next section.

There are, however, a number of recorded instances where God directly brings judgment on outsiders. Time after time, Ezekiel speaks of judgment, ending in each case with "and they (or ye) shall know that I am the Lord" (Ezekiel 11:10; 12:16; 14:8; 16:62; 25:7,11; 26:6; 29:9,16; 30:8,25,26; 33:29; 38:23).

Perhaps the main reason for judgment of non-Christians in the present life is for an example as in the following passage.

Now these things were our examples, to the intent we should not lust after evil things, as they also lusted.

Neither be ye idolaters, as were some of them; as it is written, The people sat down to eat and drink, and rose up to play. Neither let us commit fornication, as some of them committed, and fell in one day three and twenty thousand.

Neither let us tempt Christ, as some of them also tempted, and were destroyed of serpents. Neither murmur ye, as some of them also murmured, and were destroyed of the destroyer. Now all these things happened unto them for ensamples: and they are written for our admonition, upon whom the ends of the world are come (I Corinthians 10:6-11).

2. *Suffering Indirectly From God*

Much of the pain and suffering is the natural result of a fallen world and is not due to a direct act of God at the time. We often blame God for things He did not do. We ask such questions as, "Why did God do this?" when it is not God at all. James speaks of blaming God for things He is not directly responsible for in the following passage:

Blessed is the man that endureth temptation: for when he is tried, he shall receive the crown of life, which the Lord hath promised to them that love him.

Let no man say when he is tempted, I am tempted of God: for God cannot be tempted with evil, neither tempteth he any man.

But every man is tempted, when he is drawn away of his own lust, and enticed. Then when lust hath conceived, it bringeth forth sin: and sin, when it is finished, bringeth forth death.

Do not err, my beloved brethren. Every good gift and every perfect gift is from above, and cometh down from the Father of lights, with whom is no variableness, neither shadow of turning (James 1:12-17).

James also said:

From whence come wars and fightings among you? come they not hence, even of your lusts that war in your members? Ye lust, and have not: ye kill, and desire to have, and cannot obtain: ye fight and war, yet ye have not, because ye ask not.

Ye ask, and receive not, because ye ask amiss, that ye may consume it upon your lusts (James 4:1-3).

We see that good things come from God and evil results from lust and sin.

God told Jeremiah, "For I know the thoughts that I think toward you, saith the Lord, thoughts of peace, and not of evil, to give you an expected end" (Jeremiah 29:11).

Much suffering is directly caused by sin. Proverbs contains numerous verses contrasting the good which naturally results from a godly life with the evil which naturally results from sin. Many psychosomatic illnesses are caused by sinful attitudes. The Psalms contain many instances of this.

However, much suffering is brought about by the sin of others or is the natural result of a sinful world. As a result of original sin, not only man but the whole earth was cursed (Genesis 3:16-19; 5:29).

In Chapter 2, we spoke of earth as a place where we are put for just a moment to make a choice. Man chose to sin, and all suffering on earth results from that choice. We might say then that the earth is a perfect place. It's a perfect place to decide that we had better trust God because we can see what happens when we try to run things our way. As Paul said in the Scripture quoted above, any suffering a Christian endures is not worthy to be compared to the glory which will be revealed. A songwriter expressed it—"It will be worth it all when we see Jesus."

If you are interested in a philosophical approach to the problem of pain, both human and animal, of evil, and hell, I suggest you read *The Problem of Pain* by C. S. Lewis. In the present work we are considering only how the eternal view applies to the problem.

We cannot always tell whether a particular painful experience is directly caused by God for chastening or whether it is just a result of a sinful world. The Bible does, however, tell us how to respond and this will be discussed next.

Response to Suffering

Though God does not directly cause all suffering, He can use all suffering. Paul said, "And we know that all things work together for good to them that love God, to them who are the called according to his purpose" (Romans 8:28). What is His purpose? That we might "be conformed to the image of his Son" (verse 29).

In order to get the most benefit possible from our suffering, the following steps are suggested.

1. *Make Sure of Your Salvation*
This will be discussed in the chapter on faith.

2. *Check Your Life for Sin*
Unconfessed sin in your life might be the cause of your problems because of the Lord's chastening or disciplinary measures.

If you are guilty of known sin, repent and confess. Remember, "If we confess our sins, he is faithful and just to forgive us our sins, and to cleanse us from all unrighteousness" (I John 1:9).

3. *Recognize That Suffering Tests our Faith*

If our faith is being tested, we should persevere—continue striving in spite of difficulties. James said, "Blessed is the man that endureth temptation: for when he is tried, he shall receive the crown of life, which the Lord hath promised to them that love him" (James 1:12).

4. *Discover Ways to use Your Predicament as a Growing and Learning Experience*

Look again at Romans 5:3-5 and James 1:2-4 in the present context.

And not only so, but we glory in tribulations also: knowing that tribulation worketh patience; and patience, experience; and experience, hope: and hope maketh not ashamed; because the love of God is shed abroad in our hearts by the Holy Ghost which is given unto us (Romans 5:3-5).

My brethren, count it all joy when ye fall into divers temptations; knowing this, that the trying of your faith worketh patience. But let patience have her perfect work, that ye may be perfect and entire, wanting nothing (James 1:2-4).

Suffering doesn't necessarily produce growth. Tammy, a counselor at Look-Up Lodge, told that she and her sister had been nominal church members. When the girls were in their teens, their father died. The experience led Tammy to make a real commitment to the Lord. Her sister, however, turned from the Lord.

Jesus said that some "in time of temptation fall away" because they "have no firm root" (Luke 8:13). Or, in the words of Mark, "when affliction or persecution ariseth for the word's sake" they fall away (Mark 4:17).

What we suffer is not as important as how we react to it. We need to ask God to make us aware of what He wants to teach us through our sufferings.

5. *Share our Comfort With Others*

Paul said, "Blessed be God, even the Father of our Lord Jesus Christ, the Father of mercies, and the God of all comfort; who comforteth us in all our tribulation, that we may be able to comfort them which are in any trouble, by the comfort wherewith we ourselves are comforted of God (II Corinthians 1:3-4).

People who are suffering will listen to another person who has suffered in a similar situation. We should be open to opportunities to share the comfort we received from Christ.

6. *Humble Ourselves and Depend Completely on Christ*

Following the passage quoted above, Paul continued by saying:

> For we would not, brethren, have you ignorant of our trouble which came to us in Asia, that we were pressed out of measure, above

strength, insomuch that we despaired even of life: but we had the sentence of death in ourselves, that we should not trust in ourselves, but in God which raiseth the dead (II Corinthians 1:8-9).

A little later Paul said:

And lest I should be exalted above measure through the abundance of the revelations, there was given to me a thorn in the flesh, the messenger of Satan to buffet me, lest I should be exalted above measure.

For this thing I besought the Lord thrice, that it might depart from me. And he said unto me, My grace is sufficient for thee: for my strength is made perfect in weakness. Most gladly therefore will I rather glory in my infirmities, that the power of Christ may rest upon me.

Therefore I take pleasure in infirmities, in reproaches, in necessities, in persecutions, in distresses for Christ's sake: for when I am weak, then am I strong (II Corinthians 12:7-10).

7. *Recognize That no Temptation Will be too Great*
Paul said:

There hath no temptation taken you but such as is common to man: but God is faithful, who will not suffer you to be tempted above that ye are able; but will with the temptation also make a way to escape, that ye may be able to bear it (I Corinthians 10:13).

8. *Pray*

In the time of our need we can pray in the name of Jesus, knowing that He can sympathize with our weaknesses, because He was tempted in all things just as we are, yet He was without sin (Hebrews 4:15-16).

9. *Recognize the Brevity of Life and see Suffering in its Eternal Context*

This was discussed at the beginning of this chapter.

10. *Rejoice*

Beloved, think it not strange concerning the fiery trial which is to try you, as though some strange thing happened unto you: but rejoice, inasmuch as ye are partakers of Christ's sufferings; that, when his glory shall be revealed, ye may be glad also with exceeding joy. If ye be reproached for the name of Christ, happy are ye, for the spirit of glory and of God resteth upon you: on their part he is evil spoken of, but on your part he is glorified (I Peter 4:12-13).

5
Faith, Hope

Suppose you gathered a hundred seashells and only had room to take three home. Would you spend more time cleaning and polishing the three you planned to keep or the ninety-seven that would be discarded?

The Bible says that faith, hope, and love will abide (I Corinthians 13:13). Therefore, as we prepare for eternity, it would make sense to give special attention to these. While many other things in our lives will pass away, these will last.

Faith, hope, and love are often linked in the Bible and are interdependent. Works without these three have no eternal value. For example, the Thessalonians (I Thessalonians 1:1-3) and the Ephesians (Revelation 2:1-5) both had works, labor, and patience. Note the comparison below.

I Thessalonians 1:3	Revelation 2:2
Remembering without ceasing your work of faith, and labour of love, and patience of hope.	I know thy works, and thy labour, and thy patience.

However, although they both had works, labor, and patience, the first was praised and the latter was rebuked and called to repentance. Why? What was missing at Ephesus? Faith, hope, and love.

Jesus said:

Nevertheless I have somewhat against thee, because thou has left thy first love. Remember therefore from whence thou art fallen, and repent, and do the first works; or else I will come unto thee quickly, and will remove thy candlestick out of his place, except thou repent (Revelation 2:4-5).

Because of their individual importance and worth, let's look at each of these in turn.

Faith

Although love is the greatest virtue (I Corinthians 13:13), faith is the foundation on which both hope and love are built.

A. J. Gordon said:

Love comes with full hands bringing something to God; Hope comes with outstretched hands expecting something yet to be given from God; Faith comes with empty hands to receive something which has already been given by God. Therefore, since it is necessary that we receive before we give, Faith must come first, however welcome her sister graces may be afterwards. For let it be distinctly recognized that Faith originates nothing; she only recognizes what is and receives it on the soul's behalf *(Great Pulpit Masters)*.

Faith must come first because it is by faith that we are saved. A genuine salvation experience resulting from true faith will result in our becoming God's workmanship. Our good works, including love, result from His work in us.

Those who do not have faith in Jesus will not be in heaven at all, much less share in the rewards and joys discussed earlier. The sections on hope and love will show how they depend on the foundation of faith.

Biblical faith, simply put, is believing God's revelation enough to act on it. It involves confidence both in the promises of God and in the instructions of God. Lack of action distinguishes much of what is today called faith from Biblical faith.

In Chapter 2, the worthiness of rewards as motivation was discussed. But the effectiveness of the eternal view in motivating people was not discussed. We must now face the question, *"Do heavenly promises really motivate people?"* Will something in the future which cannot be seen affect people as much as things and people they see every day?

All too often the answer to the above question is no. "Few there be that find it," said Jesus of the narrow road that leads to life (Matthew 7:14). Why? Most do not have Biblical faith. Jesus said, "When the Son of man cometh, shall he find faith on the earth?" (Luke 18:8b).

The word faith and associated words such as believe and trust are used throughout the Bible. One chapter, Hebrews 11, is devoted to explaining what God means when He uses the term. Many entire books have been written on faith. Here we will concentrate on the aspects of faith related to the subject of this book.

Hebrews 11 begins by relating faith to the promises of God concerning the future. It is made abundantly clear that Biblical faith makes the future real and strongly influences our day-to-day life. The first and sixth verses spell this out as follows:

> Now faith is the substance of things hoped for, the evidence of things not seen (verse 1).
> But without faith it is impossible to please him: for he that cometh to God must believe that he is, and that he is a rewarder of them that diligently seek him (verse 6).

God says that there are two things we must believe in order to have a faith that pleases God.

The first thing we must believe is that God exists. According to polls, an overwhelming majority of American people believe that. Does that mean the majority of people in America are saved? No! Because they do not believe the second thing this passage says we must believe—that God is a rewarder of those who diligently seek Him.

How do we know most people don't believe this? Because if they did they would be diligently seeking Him. Remember the illustration in

Chapter 1 about investing a dollar in order to get a hundred dollars in return? If you didn't invest the dollar, wouldn't that be proof that you didn't have faith in the one who promised a $100 return? We need to examine our faith in the light of Hebrews 11:1, stating that faith makes the promises of God real; and Hebrews 11:6, stating that He is a rewarder of those who diligently seek Him.

The story is told of a little girl who was very frightened by a terrible thunderstorm. As the lightning and the thunder roared, the little girl's mother told her to go upstairs to bed. The little girl said she was afraid. Her mother said, "Don't worry, God will be up there with you." But the little girl said, "I want somebody with skin on." Most of us can sympathize with the little girl. It is hard for things we can't see to be as real to us as what we can see and touch. Biblical faith, however, makes the unseen things real.

Suppose we visit a tribe where money is completely unknown. We try to enlist someone to work for us and flash a $100 bill to entice them. The native would see it only as a piece of paper of no value to him. The $100 bill would be of value only to those who had faith that it was more than a piece of paper. The Bible is only a piece of paper unless we have a faith that makes the promises as real as what we can see and touch.

The faithful of Hebrews 11 not only believed in the future but they believed in obeying the commands of God in the present. Look at some examples.

Verse 7 says Noah prepared an ark by faith. Would he have been saved by a faith which said, "God, I know you told me to build an ark, but a preacher friend of mine told me a hospital would be much more relevant to the needs of our day"? No, he was saved by a faith that led him to build an ark because God said to build an ark.

Verse 17 says Abraham, by faith, offered Isaac. Would he have been saved by a faith that said, "God, I know You told me to offer Isaac, but it is neither the reasonable nor the loving thing to do. Besides, You told me the whole world would be blessed through my descendants and he's the only one I have"? No, Abraham was saved by a faith that led him to put Isaac on the altar and to carry through until God stopped him.

Verse 29 says Moses' people passed through the Red Sea by faith. Would they have been saved by a faith that said, "God, You told us to go through the Red Sea, but authorities tell us that we will get awful wet if we go that way. Now we have faith in You, but we are going to try another way"? No, they were saved by a faith that led them to do what God said.

Contrast the heroes of faith in Hebrews 11 with those who are conspicuous by their absence—those who were lost for lack of faith.

Adam and Eve disobeyed for lack of faith. This does not mean they did not believe in the existence of God. They did. They had spoken with Him often. But God said, "Don't eat that fruit," and they ate it anyway. They didn't have faith to do what God told them to do. (In His mercy God provided by way of sacrifice a covering for them to restore fellowship between them and God—a picture of salvation. But they suffered great loss because of their lack of faith.)

The rich young ruler (Matthew 19; Mark 10; Luke 18) was lost because of lack of faith (unless he later repented). He had faith enough to believe that Jesus had the key to eternal life and faith enough so he said, to keep all the commandments.

But Jesus said to him, "If you wish to be perfect, go and sell all that you have and give to the poor, and you shall have treasure in heaven; and come, follow Me." When the young ruler heard this, he went away sorrowful for he owned much property (see Matthew 19:21-22). He was lost because he didn't have faith to do what Jesus told him to do. Apparently the promised treasure in heaven was not as real as his earthly riches.

People often excuse their failure to obey by saying, "Everybody sins; nobody is perfect." But the Bible distinguishes between willful, deliberate sins and sins that are not deliberate (Hebrews 10:26). Paul describes his continuing problems with sin and the flesh as follows:

For I know that in me (that is, in my flesh,) dwelleth no good thing: for to will is present with me; but how to perform that which is good I find not. For the good that I would I do not: but the evil which I would not, that I do (Romans 7:18-19).

Note that while he continues to sin, he does not wish or will to sin.

If we had faith in the real God—the One wise and powerful enough to create the entire universe—the One who loved us enough to die for us—the One who takes such individual interest in us that He keeps up with every hair on our head, then we would want to obey Him. We would believe that His wisdom and knowledge were infinitely superior to ours, and therefore we would much rather trust Him than ourselves.

That is why John can say, "He that saith, I know him, and keepeth not his commandments, is a liar, and the truth is not in him" (I John 2:4).

How do we get the kind of faith these recorded in the faith chapter had? Actually, we have a much better opportunity than they did. This is made plain in the last two verses of the faith chapter: "And these all having obtained a good report through faith, received not the promise: God having provided some better thing for us, that they without us should not be made perfect" (Hebrews 11:39-40).

We have Jesus, who is called in Hebrews 12:2, "the author and finisher [perfecter] of our faith." It is in Him that we find the source of our faith, the object of our faith, and the enabling power for our faith.

We will talk about the enabling power later, but for now let's remember that the instrument for power which the Holy Spirit will use is the Word of God (Ephesians 6:17). Paul wrote, "So then faith cometh by hearing, and hearing by the Word of God"(Romans 10:17). The more we saturate our minds with the Word of God, the more real the promises of the Bible will become.

Suppose a person spends 16 hours a day filling his mind with things of the world and five minutes a day in God's Word. We could certainly expect the things of the world to be more real to him than the things of God.

The Bible says, "Be not deceived: God is not mocked: for whatsoever a man soweth, that shall he also reap. For he that soweth to his flesh shall of the flesh reap corruption: but he that soweth to the Spirit shall of the Spirit reap life everlasting" (Galatians 6:7-8).

The eternal life spoken of is not just something that we will get in the future. When we think in eternal terms, eternal life is something we have now (John 6:47).

Many church members sow to the flesh six days a week, then go to church on Sunday and pray for crop failure. They pray that all the worldly seed they have sown during the week will not produce. They pray that, instead, they will reap a spiritual harvest, though little spiritual seed was sown.

Peter said, "As newborn babes, desire the sincere milk of the word, that ye may grow thereby" (I Peter 2:2). Our faith grows as we feed on the Word.

Prayer is another means of exercising our faith. A prayer we could all pray is, "Lord, I believe; help thou mine unbelief" (Mark 9:24b). Or, in the words of the apostles, "Increase our faith" (Luke 17:5).

Bible study and prayer are not enough, however. We must act on the faith we already have. As we exercise our faith, it will grow. This is illustrated in the life of Naaman (II Kings 5).

Captain of the army of Syria, Naaman was also a leper. As a result of the witness of a servant girl from Israel, he went to the Prophet Elisha to be healed. Through a messenger, Elisha instructed Naaman to wash in the Jordan seven times and he would be healed.

After first refusing out of anger, he finally gave in and did what the man of God had told him to do. This took a certain amount of faith because he was subjecting himself to all kinds of ridicule if it didn't work. Imagine how people would have taunted him. "Hey, Naaman, taken any baths lately?" "Did you really think that water would heal you?" Naaman must have had doubts but he acted on the faith he had.

God healed him and he said, "Behold, now I know that there is no God in all the earth, but in Israel" (II Kings 5:15). He had acted on his faith and, thus, received even more faith.

Exercising faith can be compared with learning to walk. At first, a child finds walking very difficult. But the more he walks, the easier it becomes and soon he reaches the point where he walks without even thinking about it.

Paul said that "we walk by faith" (II Corinthians 5:7). The more we walk by faith, the easier it becomes.

Bible study, prayer, and exercise cannot develop fully without the enabling power of the Holy Spirit. Consider the following passage:

> But as it is written, Eye hath not seen, nor ear heard, neither have entered into the heart of man, the things which God hath prepared for them that love him. But God hath revealed them unto us by his Spirit: for the Spirit searcheth all things, yea, the deep things of God.
>
> For what man knoweth the things of a man, save the spirit of man which is in him? even so the things of God knoweth no man, but the Spirit of God. Now we have received, not the spirit of the world, but the spirit which is of God; that we might know the things that are

freely given to us of God. Which things also we speak, not in the words which man's wisdom teacheth, but which the Holy Ghost teacheth; comparing spiritual things with spiritual.

But the natural man receiveth not the things of the Spirit of God: for they are foolishness unto him: neither can he know them, because they are spiritually discerned. But he that is spiritual judgeth all things, yet he himself is judged of no man. For who hath known the mind of the Lord, that he may instruct him? But we have the mind of Christ (I Corinthians 2:9-16).

In verses 9 and 10 above we find that the things God has prepared for those who love Him are revealed through the Spirit. Verse 14 tells us that it is foolishness to the natural man.

Even when we have been born again, remember that we are born as babes. Since becoming a Christian, have you ever worried about something that would not make a bit of difference a hundred years from now? So have I. We need to grow in the Spirit.

The discussion about faith thus far has been for those who already believe the essential facts about Christ and who accept the authority of the Bible. Most readers would fall into this category, since there would be little point in reading this book otherwise. Evidences for faith are therefore not discussed here to any great length. Those who have doubts about the basics should read a book dealing with this subject. I recommend *Know Why You Believe* by Paul Little, *Evidence that Demands a Verdict* by Josh McDowell, or *Mere Christianity* by C. S. Lewis. You will find that there is much more evidence for Biblical faith than there is for any other option.

This does not mean that the evidence found in these books or any other book can convince a person who doesn't want to believe. For example, Christians who have examined the overwhelming evidences for the bodily resurrection of Christ often wonder why non-Christians can't see it. Why can some who even call themselves Christians make statements such as, "All scholars agree that the resurrection is a myth"? It all depends on our presuppositions.

Perhaps we can understand doubters if we look at a situation where we doubt what appears to be solid evidence because of our presuppositions. Suppose a stage magician shows us an apparently empty hat. He utters some magic words and lo—out of the hat comes a rabbit. Are we convinced that he was able to create the rabbit by magic? Of course not. Though all the evidence indicates that he did, our presuppositions tell us that no man can create a rabbit.

We could therefore say that all scholars agree that there was no magic, simply a trick. Anyone who claimed the rabbit was produced by magic would not meet our definition of "scholar" and would be dismissed as one who let his superstitions overrule his reasoning.

Atheists and so-called liberal Christians often begin with the presupposition that miracles don't happen—that men dead three days don't rise again. Therefore, the evidence that Jesus did rise from the dead will not convince them. "We can't explain it, but there must have been a trick."

Evidence, therefore, cannot convince one who doesn't want to be convinced. A study of evidence can, however, show that you don't have to commit intellectual suicide in order to become a Christian.

If you really want to know God, you can find Him. The Bible says that you will seek Him and find Him, when you search for Him with all your heart (Jeremiah 29:13).

Unbelief results more from an unwillingness to submit than from intellectual hangups. There is ample evidence for faith in the books previously mentioned for anyone who will seek with an open mind.

If you have any doubt about your salvation, follow Paul's admonition to "examine yourselves, whether ye be in the faith; prove your own selves. Know ye not your own selves, how that Jesus Christ is in you, except ye be reprobates?" (II Corinthians 13:5).

How can you know? John said, "These things have I written unto you that believe on the name of the Son of God; that ye may know that ye have eternal life" (I John 5:13). When John said "These things have I written," he was referring to the entire letter. Since the letter is quite short, read it through and put a "T" in the margin by any verse that gives a test of your salvation. You should be able to group these tests under three headings:

(1) Moral—Do you desire to keep His commandments?

(2) Social—Do you love others?

(3) Theological—Do you believe the correct things about Christ?

We should emphasize that none of the above save you but are tests of a genuine salvation experience resulting from receiving Jesus by faith as Lord and Saviour.

If you are not sure you have real faith, take time right now to make sure. If you are sure of your salvation, train diligently to increase your faith. Since faith is one of the things that will abide forever, one of the most profitable things we can do is practice thinking and acting from the point of view of faith.

Closely connected to faith is hope, the second abiding virtue.

Hope

Paul prayed for understanding of hope for the Ephesians, that they might know the hope of His calling, and what the riches of the glory that were to be theirs (Ephesians 1:18).

Contrast this to those "having no hope, and without God in the world" (Ephesians 2:12).

Peter said, "Blessed be the God and Father of our Lord Jesus Christ, who, according to his abundant mercy, hath begotten us again unto a lively [living] hope by the resurrection of Jesus Christ from the dead, to an inheritance incorruptible, and undefiled, and that fadeth not away, reserved in heaven for you" (I Peter 1:3-4).

Note that only those who have been born again have any hope—and that hope is in heaven. Paul said, "If in this life only we have hope in Christ, we are of all men most miserable" (I Corinthians 15:19). The hope is laid up for us in heaven (Colossians 1:5).

Biblical hope is not a desire for something that may or may not happen. Faith makes our hope sure (Hebrews 11:1). Our hope is based on God who cannot lie (Titus 1:2); it is "an anchor of the soul" (Hebrew 6:19).

An illustration of hope as a mere wish and hope based upon fact occurred in Tennessee recently. Shortly before leaving office, Governor Blanton pardoned a large number of men who were in prison for life.

Before receiving word of the pardon, the men doubtlessly hoped that something would occur that would result in their release. However, since the chances were slim, most of their thoughts and efforts concerned prison life. They were concerned with getting good prison jobs, being accepted by the right crowd of inmates, and making prison life as comfortable and pleasant as possible.

Then word of the pardon came. While waiting for the papers to come through, they were still in the same prison, but their thoughts had changed. What would they do on the outside? What kind of life would they have there?

Though physically still in prison they no longer thought of themselves as prisoners, but as free men. The discomforts of prison were no longer a major concern. Knowledge that the release papers had already been signed gave them a hope which changed their entire outlook. Hope based on fact doubtlessly produced a change which hope as a wish could never have done.

Suppose that one of the pardoned prisoners had previously received word that he had inherited, in trust, a nice home, a new automobile, and a boat. What value would these have for a man in prison for life? But when his hope for release was made sure by the governor's signature, those possessions on the outside suddenly became extremely valuable.

A hope for heavenly rewards which is a vague desire will not affect our lives as much as a true Biblical hope.

How do we get this hope? Paul tells us:

For whatsoever things were written afore-
time were written for our learning, that we
through patience and comfort of the scriptures
might have hope.

Now the God of hope fill you with all joy and
peace in believing, that ye may abound in
hope, through the power of the Holy Ghost
(Romans 15:4, 13).

Thus, the Scriptures, faith, and the power of
the Holy Spirit are necessary to produce hope.

Our hope is not dependent upon ourselves—
our own feeble efforts—or outer circumstances.
Our hope centers in Christ (Colossians 1:26-27).

Not only do we have hope because Christ is in
us now, we have hope because of His assured
return. We are "looking for that blessed hope, and
the glorious appearing of the great God and our
Saviour, Jesus Christ" (Titus 2:13).

Hope is connected with both faith and love in
many Scriptures. Therefore, hope is not selfish.
What we hope for ourselves, we also hope for
others. This is an important motive for witnessing. Just as a farmer sows and plows because he
has hope of reaping, we sow spiritual seed and
cultivate prospects because we have hope for
them.

How should hope affect our lives now? The
Bible mentions several things that should result
from true hope.

1. *Purity*

John said, "And every man that hath this hope in him purifieth himself, even as he is pure" (I John 3:3). To get this passage in context, look at the verses preceeding it.

Behold, what manner of love the Father hath bestowed upon us, that we should be called the sons of God: therefore the world knoweth us not, because it knew him not. Beloved, now are we the sons of God, and it doth not yet appear what we shall be: but we know that, when he shall appear, we shall be like him; for we shall see him as he is (I John 3:1-2).

We see that because of love God made us sons, and because we are sons we will be like Jesus. This is the hope that leads to purity.

2. *Witnessing*

We have already said that the hope we have for others should lead us to witness. Paul compared preaching the gospel to sowing in I Corinthians 9:10-11. Jesus also spoke of sowing the Word in Luke 8:11-15. Though most of the seed fell on soil that did not produce, some fell on good soil which brought forth an abundant harvest. This harvest made the sowing worthwhile.

3. *Charitable Giving*

Paul again uses the analogy of sowing and reaping in II Corinthians 9:6, but this time in the context of giving. In pleading with the Corinthians to give generously, he said: "But this I say, He which soweth sparingly shall reap also sparingly; and he which soweth bountifully shall reap also bountifully" (II Corinthians 9:6).

4. *Joy*

Paul said, "Now the God of hope fill you with all joy" (Romans 15:13). In Romans 12:12, he spoke of "rejoicing in hope." Hebrews 3:6 also speaks of "the rejoicing of the hope." One of the great causes of sadness and depression is lack of hope. We can think of many examples of people who are without human hope: invalids, terminally ill patients, prisoners, poverty stricken people, the elderly. However, a Christian is never without hope. The closer he is to death, the closer he is to the fulfillment of his hope.

5. *Patience*

Paul refers to the "patience of hope in our Lord Jesus Christ" (I Thessalonians 1:3). We have the hope that He who has begun a good work in us will complete it (Philippians 1:6) and that one day He will present us blameless before the presence of His glory (Jude 24). It should, therefore, be easier for us to be patient with ourselves and with fellow Christians.

Hope should not only lead to patience with people but should lead to patience in tribulation. Tribulation leads to patience and hope. Paul said, "And not only so, but we glory in tribulations also: knowing that tribulation worketh patience;

and patience, experience; and experience, hope" (Romans 5:3-4).

Like spiral stairs which go round and round, continually rising, these virtues reinforce each other on an ever higher level. Hope leads to joy in tribulation which strengthens our patience which produces greater hope which leads to more joy in tribulation, and on and on.

6. *Diligence in Ministering*

The Bible says, "For God is not unrighteous to forget your work and labour of love, which ye have shewed toward his name, in that ye have ministered to the saints, and do minister. And we desire that every one of you do show the same diligence to the full assurance of hope unto the end" (Hebrews 6:10-11). Note in the above passage that hope and love work together to produce diligence in ministering to fellow Christians.

7. *Anchor for the Soul*

Midst the storms and uncertainties of this life, our hope serves as "an anchor of the soul, a hope both sure and stedfast" (Hebrews 6:19). We need not be like "children, tossed to and fro, and carried about with every wind of doctrine" (Ephesians 4:14).

8. *Helmet*

Paul told us to put on for a "helmet, the hope of salvation" (I Thessalonians 5:8). Satan is called "the accuser of our brethren" (Revelation 12:10).

One of his weapons in the spiritual warfare is to make us doubt our salvation, to lead us to believe that we are not good enough to serve or that our faith won't last. However, since our hope is not in ourselves but in Christ, since we do not depend on our ability to hold out but on His ability to keep us (II Timothy 1:12), we have the means to win over Satan.

9. *Be Ready to Give Reason*

Peter said, "But sanctify the Lord God in your hearts: and be ready always to give an answer to every man that asketh you a reason of the hope that is in you with meekness and fear" (I Peter 3:15).

Since hope is so important to Christians, and since it is so needed by the lost, we should study diligently in order to be able to explain the reason for the hope we have. Our hope is not a blind leap in the dark but is based on solid evidence, including the historical fact of the resurrection of Jesus. As has been said before, there is much more evidence for Christianity than for any alternate view of existence, but, we need to know the evidence in order to follow the Biblical command to be able to give reasons for our hope.

6
The Greatest Is Love

The importance of faith has been discussed. Remember, however, that the Bible says, "And though I have all faith, so that I could remove mountains, and have not charity, I am nothing." In fact, everything we have talked about thus far is useless without love, as we see in the following excerpt from I Corinthians 13:

Though I speak with the tongues of men and of angels, and have not charity [love], I am become as sounding brass, or a tinkling cymbal. And though I have the gift of prophecy, and understand all mysteries, and all knowledge; and though I have all faith, so that I could remove mountains, and have not charity, I am nothing. And though I bestow all my goods to feed the poor, and though I give my body to be burned, and have not charity, it profiteth me nothing (I Corinthians 13:1-3).

Suffering and persecution are sometimes unavoidable, even desirable as an example, but the Bible says, "If I deliver my body to be burned, but do not have love, it profits me nothing." We speak of laying up treasures in heaven by giving to the poor, but must remember that if we give all our possessions to feed the poor . . . and have not love, it profits us nothing.

Paul said, "And now abideth faith, hope, charity, these three; but the greatest of these is charity" (I Corinthians 13:13). Love for God and love for our neighbors were emphasized by Jesus as the greatest commandments.

Because love is the greatest virtue, however, many make the mistake of trying to make it the fundamental virtue. But the fundamental virtue must be faith. Love that is not built on the proper foundation of faith is vain. Love is the first fruit of the Spirit (Galatians 5:22). But we cannot produce the fruit of the Spirit until we are born of the Spirit. And we are not born of the Spirit until we receive Jesus by faith (John 1:12-13).

The word "love" is used to cover a wide variety of things, but we are speaking here of "agape" love as defined in I Corinthians 13. Agape love considers the object of love to be infinitely precious. Agape desires the very best for the one loved. It is a self-sacrificing love.

This kind of love is humanly impossible. John said, "Love is of God; and every one that loveth is born of God" (I John 4:7b) which shows two things: those truly born of God will love, and only those who are born of God *can* love.

Since Biblical love is not natural, we can only love when Christ puts His nature in us. The correct order is given in II Peter 1:4-7. We first become partakers of the divine nature by faith. Then, to our faith we add a series of virtues, building one upon the other, until we come to the top which is love.

The correct order—beginning with faith and proceeding through hope and other virtues to love—is also found in Romans 5:1-5 (emphasis added) as follows:

Therefore being justified by
                FAITH,
we have peace with God through our Lord
Jesus Christ: by whom also we have access by
                FAITH
into this grace wherein we stand, and rejoice
in
                HOPE
of the glory of God. And not only so, but we
glory in tribulations also: knowing that tribulation worketh patience; and patience, experience; and experience,
                HOPE;
and hope maketh not ashamed; because the
                LOVE
of God is shed abroad in our hearts by the Holy
Ghost which is given unto us.

Note in verse 5 that it is God's love through
the Holy Spirit. God knows how pitifully little
love we can generate within ourselves so He
sheds His own love through us.

Any attempt to reverse the order results in
failure. Oh, some appear to show great love for
awhile. They may even give all their goods to
feed the poor, but still be lacking agape love, as
we saw in I Corinthians 13:3. Much of what
passes for love is really an attempt to meet some

subconscious psychological need and has no eternal value.

Errors of Fake Love

Love that is not based on faith not only lacks genuineness, but it leads to serious errors and wasted effort. Some of the errors are discussed below.

1. *Misdirected Zeal*

Who would have been showing more realistic love on the sinking Titanic? A man who was painting the ship and trying to make it more pleasant, or one who was preparing the lifeboats and urging people to get into them?

Many people direct their zeal toward making this life more pleasant for others and fail to prepare them for eternity. Our deeds should be in proper perspective. As we shall see shortly, the right kind of love, based on real faith, should lead to social action. However, we should realize that the most loving thing we can do for anyone is to lead him into a right relationship with Jesus.

2. *Affirming People in Sin*

Another error some make in the name of love is to affirm people in their sin. Suppose you saw two friends paddling down a river in a canoe. You knew they would shortly come to a steep waterfall where they would plunge to their death.

What would be the loving thing to do? Would you say, "If I yelled at them, it would upset them. They are having a very happy time and I don't want to do anything to interfere. Besides, I go the wrong direction sometimes myself." No, the loving thing would be to say, "Stop! Turn around! Go the other way!"

In determining whether to affirm or rebuke, we need to discern whether or not the sin is willful. If it is not deliberate rebellion against God, we approach our brothers as in Galatians 6:1-2:

> Brethren, if a man be overtaken in a fault, ye which are spiritual, restore such an one in the spirit of meekness; considering thyself, lest thou also be tempted. Bear ye one another's burdens, and so fulfil the law of Christ.

If we detect deliberate sin, we follow Paul's admonition to "Preach the word; be instant in season, out of season; reprove, rebuke, exhort with all longsuffering and doctrine. For the time will come when they will not endure sound doctrine; but after their own lusts shall they heap to themselves teachers, having itching ears" (II Timothy 4:2-3).

3. *Failure to Get to the Root*

Evangelicals are often criticized because they "harp on" things such as drinking and adultery and preach gospel messages instead of helping the poor. It is interesting, though, that a Salvation Army officer who spends most of his time working with the poor says that well over 90 percent of the poverty he sees is directly due to sin, primarily the sins of drunkenness and adultery. Since these sins are "works of the flesh" (Galatians 5:19-21), the only lasting solution is to lead men to be born of the Spirit and then to walk in the Spirit.

We should not, therefore, criticize people for preaching the gospel and for preaching against sin. We should realize, however, that if this is all they do, they have not gone far enough.

4. *Wrong Political Solutions*

A concern for others which is not based on faith in God's assessment of man will lead to wrong political solutions. Failure to recognize the innate sinfulness of human nature could lead us to move left toward communism or socialism, or right toward something like Nazism. Both result from a false view of human nature.

Communism assumes that man is basically good and that if he were not oppressed by capitalists, he would naturally be unselfish. Therefore, he would work according to his ability and receive according to his need. Sounds great—if it were not for the basic sin nature of man. There are some "workaholics" who work because of an inner need or compulsion. However, most will work for one of two reasons—they are rewarded if they do or punished if they don't.

Free enterprise is based on the reward motive. A man who achieves more should get more. Communism is based, theoretically, on the belief that man is basically good and therefore should need neither rewards nor punishment as motivation. That is why communist doctrine teaches that no policemen would be needed in a communist state. The fallacy should be obvious as the communist countries have become the tightest police states in the world.

Nazism and similar governments have taken a different approach. Recognizing the evils of freedom, they concentrate power in the hands of a few "wise" people who will do what is best for the country. The problem is that the one or few at the top are also sinners.

Situation Ethics

Situation ethics is one of the most dangerous results of putting love on a pedestal without an underlying faith in the Word of God. Before discussing this further, let me say that all ethics is "situation" ethics, but I am discussing a certain group of presuppositions that has come to be called "situation ethics." Just as I belong to the church of Christ but do not belong to the particular denomination which calls itself the Church of Christ, so I believe in situation ethics but not in the view that is called Situation Ethics.

145

Below are listed some of the basic teachings of situation ethics as stated by Joseph Fletcher, one of its leading spokesmen, in his book entitled *Situation Ethics:*

Situation ethics . . . rejecting all "revealed" norms or laws but the one command—to love God and the neighbor . . . Only the command to love is categorically good. "Owe no one anything, except to love one another" (Rom. 13:8). (P. 26)

The First Proposition: "Only one 'thing' is intrinsically good; namely love: nothing else at all." (P. 59)

The Second Proposition: "The ruling norm of Christian decision is love; nothing else." (P. 69)

A young unmarried couple might decide, if they make their decision Christianly, to have intercourse (e.g., by getting pregnant to force a selfish parent to relent his overbearing resistance to their marriage). But as Christians they would never say, "It's all right if we like each other!" Loving concern can make it all right, but mere like cannot. (P. 104)

The Christian ethic is not interested in reluctant virgins and technical chastity. What sex probably needs more than anything is a good airing, demythologizing it and getting rid of its mystique-laden and occult accretions, which come from romanticism on the one hand and puritanism on the other. People are learning that we can have sex without love, and love without sex; that baby-making can be (and often ought to be) separated from love-making. It is, indeed, for re-creation as well as for pro-creation. But if people do not believe it is wrong to have sex relations outside marriage, it isn't, unless they hurt themselves, their partners, or others. This is, of course, a very big "unless" and gives reason to many to abstain altogether except within the full mutual commitment of marriage. The civil lawmakers are rapidly ridding their books of statutes making unmarried sex a crime between consenting adults. All situationists would agree with Mrs. Patrick Campbell's remark that they can do what they want "as long as they don't do it in the street and frighten the horses." (P. 140)

Note that Fletcher quoted from Romans 13:8, but he stopped short. Let's examine the passage in context:

Owe no man anything, but to love one another: for he that loveth another hath fulfilled the law. For this, Thou shalt not commit adultery, Thou shalt not kill, Thou shalt not steal, Thou shalt not bear false witness, Thou shalt not covet; and if there be any other commandment, it is briefly comprehended in this saying, namely, Thou shalt love thy neighbour as thyself. Love worketh no ill to his neighbour: therefore love is the fulfilling of the law (Romans 13:8-10).

The problem with using love as the only guide is that, if we ignore the Word of God, we are left to decide what the loving thing is with our "flesh." Paul said, "For I know that in me (that is, in my flesh,) dwelleth no good thing" (Romans 7:18). He also said, "Now the works of the flesh are manifest, which are these; Adultery, fornication, uncleanness, lasciviousness" (Galatians 5:19).

Surely our flesh will tell us that the loving thing to do with a girl is to have sex with her. This is why only that love resulting from a salvation experience and based on a firm foundation of faith in the Word of God is reliable.

I said at the beginning of this section that the Bible teaches situation ethics but not what is called Situation Ethics. That is, the Bible recognizes that there are certain exceptions to the general rule, but where this is necessary, provision is made for safeguards so that it won't be the flesh acting in the name of love.

For example, the commandment, "Thou shalt not kill" is found in Exodus 20:13. This is the rule. However, in Exodus 21, instances are given where the Israelites were actually commanded to kill (Exodus 21:12, 14-17, 29).

The point is that the entire Bible is the Word of God and no single part of it can be taken without reference to the rest. If you have read only Exodus 20, you have not heard the Word of God regarding killing. There is much more in both the Old and New Testaments.

Note also that when a man was condemned to death, it was a judicial matter with elaborate safeguards (Deuteronomy 19:15-19). It was not revenge by emotionally involved people—this would have opened it up to the works of the flesh.

We see, then, that breaking the commandment not to kill under authorization from clarifying Scriptures by those not emotionally involved is quite different from deciding to commit adultery because it is the loving thing to do. It's quite different from the couple in Mr. Fletcher's example who broke the commandment, "Thou shalt not commit adultery," in order to break another commandment, "Honour thy father and thy mother."

True Love

Let's turn now to examine true Christian love—the love that results from a genuine salvation experience and the continuing work of the Holy Spirit in our lives. We will see that true love will lead to social involvement, but without the errors mentioned previously.

Many believe that love resulting from a faith experience doesn't work because most professing evangelicals are not involved in social action with people. This is like saying that soap doesn't work because there are so many people with soap in their houses who are still dirty. It is not the fault of the soap; neither is it the fault of the gospel message. Rather, it is the lack of a proper application of both.

As we observe the failure of church members as a group to demonstrate practical love, we need to remember three things.

First, many church members are not really Christians. Remember the people of Matthew 7:21-27 who called Jesus Lord, prophesied in His name, cast out demons in His name and performed mighty miracles in His name, but were lost because they did not do the will of God? Certainly helping our fellowman is part of God's will for us.

Second, we need to remember that much of the social good that has been accomplished has been the result of evangelicals responding to the Holy Spirit. Sherwood Wirt, former editor of *Decision* magazine, said:

That the social evils of the modern era have by no means been utterly neglected by the evangelicals is a point that cannot be stated too often. Social historians are well aware that for over two hundred years, under the impetus of John Wesley and the evangelical revival, Christian eleemosynary institutions and "works of mercy" have been proliferating in Europe and America. City rescue missions, societies for the blind; hospitals, sanitaria, orphanages, homes for the aged, ragged schools, and centers of healing; YMCAs, institutions for the mentally retarded, for the blind, for fallen girls, for widows, for prisoner rehabilitation; for the protection of animals; and a host of similar operations came into being to meet the growing needs *(The Social Conscience of the Evangelical)*.

Third, remember that Christians have different gifts and different functions within the body (Romans 12 and I Corinthians 12). Because someone does not perform the same function we do does not mean he is not of the body.

Two loves will result if built on the proper foundation. We'll examine each in turn.

1. *Love for God*

And Jesus answered him, The first of all the commandments is, Hear, O Israel; the Lord our God is one Lord: and thou shalt love the Lord thy God with all thy heart, and with all thy soul, and with all thy mind, and with all thy strength: this is the first commandment (Mark 12:29-30).

Love for God is the response of the soul to His prior love for us. "Herein is love, not that we loved God, but that he loved us, and sent his Son to be the propitiation for our sins" (I John 4:10).

When we really comprehend the love that led Jesus to bear the full burden, guilt, punishment, and shame of our sin, our lives are changed. We realize that this love was totally undeserved. "But God commendeth his love toward us, in that, while we were yet sinners, Christ died for us" (Romans 5:8).

It was response to the love or grace of God that caused Paul to work so hard. "But by the grace of God I am what I am: and his grace which was bestowed upon me was not in vain; but I laboured more abundantly than they all: yet not I, but the grace of God which was with me" (I Corinthians 15:10). If we have experienced the same grace, it should affect us the same way.

Obviously, if we do not have faith in the actual historical demonstration of God's love on the cross, our appreciation of God's love will fall far short. Those who admire Jesus because He was unselfish and went about doing good have sensed only a small fraction of the love that caused Jesus to leave heaven, take on the limitation of a flesh-and-blood body, and carry our sins to the cross.

Unless we love the God revealed in the Scriptures, we love a false God, a projected image of our own imagination. This love of a false God will lead to a fake love for our fellowman.

True love for the true God, however, affects everything we do. In my book, *Commonsense Christianity,* I have an entire chapter, called "Married to Christ," in which I compare love for my wife with love for Jesus. Just as my love for my wife led me to want to read her love letters, spend time with her, and introduce her to my friends, our love for Jesus should make us relate to Him similarly.

As we discussed in the chapter on motivation, our love for God revealed in Christ will lead us to do what pleases Him most and to have many crowns to cast at His feet (Revelation 4:10-11). It is love for Jesus that leads to the right kind of love for our fellowman.

2. *Love for Man*

And the second is like, namely this, Thou shalt love thy neighbour as thyself. There is none other commandment greater than these (Mark 12:31).

In response to the question, "And who is my neighbor?" Jesus told the familiar story of the good Samaritan (Luke 10:29-36), concluding with, "Which now of these three, thinkest thou, was neighbour unto him that fell among the thieves? And he said, He that shewed mercy on him. Then said Jesus unto him, Go, and do thou likewise" (Luke 10:36-37).

Love is more than an emotion: it involves action. While the Bible has a lot to say about the special love we have for fellow Christians, this passage clearly teaches love for anyone we can help.

If I truly love my fellowman I will, like Jesus, have concern for both his eternal and his present well-being.

I once witnessed to a young man who was a church member and claimed to be a Christian but never attended church and had no active involvement. He said, "I believe in I Corinthians 13. If you love your fellowman, that's all that is necessary."

I said, "If there were a child lost in the woods and you loved the child, would you help find him? Would you join an organized effort to make a diligent search for him?"

He said, "Of course. I would help even if I didn't know him. I love everybody."

I said, "Suppose there is someone out there spiritually lost. Would you join an organized effort to reach him?"

"Huh, that's different."

I said, "Of course it's different. If a child is lost physically and dies, that takes 60 or 70 years off his life, and this is terrible. But if someone is lost spiritually and dies, that is forever."

We cannot claim to love people and sit idly by while they go to hell without making an effort to reach as many as we can.

But true love also leads us to be concerned for the present welfare of others. Both the Old and New Testaments abound with passages commanding a practical love which results in helping people. The Bible makes it clear in such passages as Isaiah 1:11-17 and Amos 5:21-24 that religious talk and ritual are useless without a concern for justice and mercy.

Not only are we commanded to love, but love is a test of the genuineness of our salvation experience, as is shown in the following Scriptures:

> A new commandment I give unto you, That ye love one another; as I have loved you, that ye also love one another. By this shall all men know that ye are my disciples, if ye have love one to another (John 13:34-35).

> We know that we have passed from death unto life, because we love the brethren. He that loveth not his brother abideth in death (I John 3:14).

> If a man say, I love God, and hateth his brother, he is a liar: for he that loveth not his brother whom he hath seen, how can he love God whom he hath not seen? (I John 4:20).

In addition to the explicit teachings of the Bible, we have the example of Jesus. Jesus went about doing good (Acts 10:38). If He lives in us, so will we.

While Jesus was primarily concerned with eternal values, He also displayed great concern and compassion for the present comfort and well-being of all people. He said, "This is my commandment, That ye love one another, as I have loved you" (John 15:12).

How can we love our neighbor as ourselves and as Jesus loved us? The Christian has several things going for him that a non-Christian doesn't have.

Response to God's Love

Just as our love for God results from His prior love for us, so our love for our fellowman results from God's love.

John said, "Beloved, if God so loved us, we ought also to love one another" (I John 4:11).

As we respond to the unspeakable love that God has for us, we realize that He has this same love for all. "Hereby perceive we the love of God, because he laid down his life for us: and we ought to lay down our lives for the brethren" (I John 3:16).

There is no greater favor anyone can do me than to do something nice for my wife or children. Similarly, the way to hurt me is to hurt one of my loved ones. Jesus said, "Inasmuch as ye have done it unto one of the least of these my brethren, ye have done it unto me" (Matthew 25:40b).

We have previously seen that true love is possible only by the enabling power of the Holy Spirit. But if the Spirit produces love, why don't more Christians show more love? Although all

156

Christians *have* the Holy Spirit, not all Christians *walk in the Spirit* or yield to the Spirit as much as they should.

Paul said, "This I say then, Walk in the Spirit, and ye shall not fulfil the lust of the flesh. For the flesh lusteth against the Spirit, and the Spirit against the flesh: and these are contrary the one to the other: so that ye cannot do the things that ye would" (Galatians 5:16-17).

The Christian should recognize the two forces within him and make a conscious effort to yield to the Spirit (Romans 6:12-13). Realizing that his feelings may be of the flesh, he doesn't rely on his feelings, but on faith in what God has revealed. Since God has revealed that we should act in love, a Christian proceeds to do the loving thing, regardless of his feelings.

My daughter, Carolyn, is presently involved in urban ministries with the Fellowship House in Washington, D.C. She and several other volunteers were helping with a run—down ghetto boardinghouse which had become the unofficial retirement home of about fifty people.

Many of the "guests" were former inmates of mental institutions and hospitals and had no family or friends who cared about them. The sheets had not been changed for weeks and many reeked with body elimination wastes. To say the whole place stunk is an understatement.

Week after week, the crew from the Fellowship House went to clean up the house, clean up the

157

boarders, and begin the long process of getting their records in order so they could be moved to a proper facility. Why?

On a visit to Washington, we had the opportunity to talk to Betty, the one with whom Carolyn worked most closely. She was the widow of a career army officer who had lived in a normal routine most of her life. However, a few years before our meeting someone had taught her about the Holy Spirit. She surrendered to Him and He led her into that type of ministry. Note that no one told her to be more concerned for others. That wouldn't have worked. She was led to yield to the Holy Spirit and He did the rest.

We also talked to John Staggers who was in charge of the urban ministries programs of the Fellowship House. He is a black former Professor of Sociology who has served in many responsible positions, including mayor's assistant. He told me that he was realizing more and more that, unless we lead people to a personal commitment to Christ, we are wasting our time. He said much of the welfare expenditure has been money down the drain because lasting results did not come unless people were transformed by Christ.

Summary

The double thesis of this book is that we should have our minds on eternal values and that, if we do so, we will also be of the greatest possible value in the present. We have shown that growing in the abiding virtues, faith, hope, and love, will produce an abundant life, both here and in the world to come.

I once heard a story—a fable, if you will—that helped me to get things into perspective. A man riding along on his horse came to a stream. A funny little man stepped out and said, "Get off your horse. Pick up all the pebbles you can, and tomorrow you will be both glad and sorry."

It didn't make much sense, but the traveler decided to humor the little man. He picked up a few pebbles and went on his way. The next day he understood what the man had meant. All the pebbles had changed to diamonds. He was truly both glad and sorry. He was glad he had picked up as many as he had but he was terribly sorry that he had not picked up more.

We view life in a very limited, temporary way now but there will come a day a million years from now, a billion years from now, when each one of us will look back on the life we lived in the flesh. When we do, we will be both glad and sorry. We will be so glad we did what we did and so sorry we didn't do more.